MODERN RIDING TECHNIQUES

Selma Brandl

MODERN RIDING TECHNIQUES

HARMONY IN HORSEMANSHIP

SWAN HILL
PRESS

First published in the UK in 1997 by the Swan Hill Press
an imprint of Airlife Publishing Ltd

First published in Germany in 1995 as
Die Moderne Reitschule

British Library Cataloguing in Publication Data
A catalogue record for this book
is available from the British Library

ISBN 1 85310 815 4

Typeset by Livesey Ltd, Shrewsbury, England
Printed in England

Swan Hill Press
an imprint of Airlife Publishing Ltd
101 Longden Road, Shrewsbury SY3 9EB, England

Contents

Introduction

In recent years the number of equestrian books on the market has increased enormously. Many reflect new approaches to horse-management, veterinary care, feeding and sometimes to training.

They all add to our knowledge of the horse, but we would do well to remember, in the midst of all the available instruction and advice, that the horse, which is central to all our activities, has remained essentially the same ever since man's involvement with the equine species.

The horse, indeed, is the one constant factor in what has been termed 'the equine progression'.

If the relationship between the horse and the human being is

to be a happy one and mutually fulfilling to both parties we can never afford to lose sight of that fact.

The first requirement of the human being in keeping, handling and training horses is to acquire an understanding of the nature and physiology of the horse.

Secondly, and just as importantly, the rider has to establish self-discipline over mind and body, striving consciously to work effectively in a state of mental relaxation. Clearly, also, the necessary physical ability relevant to the riding discipline has to be developed and perfected, and that is not possible without a thorough understanding of the classical theory.

Good riding and sensitive, responsible horse-management is a matter of communication between two members of a partnership – the one human, the other animal. The responsibility for its creation is that of the former and there are no short cuts.

The Nature of the Horse

When watching groups of horses in a field, we will become conscious of the nature of the horse. Harmony, calmness, composure are all words that express what every person must feel when looking at so much beauty. The symmetry of movement in horses at grass shows their ability to communicate with each other and their desire of physical contact. Bearing this in mind, a review of our modern horse keeping methods will reveal, even to a non-specialist in horses, that the domestic life imposed on the horse is scarcely in accord with the animal's nature. If we are not able to assess the horse's requirements correctly and to provide for them, it is hardly surprising if horses display their resentment and frustration in displays of bad behaviour.

There are often times when both rider and horse can stop and relax – take your time, stay still and savour the moment together.

To avoid these situations arising we have to learn to understand the language of the horse, be able to interpret any bad behaviour and apply an appropriate remedy. We must also learn to rectify our own movement and behaviour, introducing a quiet balance to the way we move about – so bringing calmness and a relaxed atmosphere to the relationship. Any agitation, hectic pace, or anything troubling us at the time must be put aside if we want to get close to our horse in a manner appropriate to its nature. Time is the greatest luxury that the horse requires of us, because 'reason, patience and time make possible the impossible' (*Goethe*).

To ride and handle a horse properly will only be possible if you know how that animal behaves. The behaviour of any living creature will stem from the space it is given: they are all equipped to survive within their own environment. Also a stabled horse will still retain the behaviour patterns of the herd animal it once was. Horses prefer to be with their own kind, so that they can hear, see, smell and, if possible, touch each other. It is thus essential for human beings to adjust themselves to the natural behaviour patterns of the horse, and this cannot be judged by the measure of human logic and human needs.

This pony, the two little girls and their dog are relaxed and in harmony with each other.

These pictures show the many different ways in which horse riding can be enjoyed and the different breeds that have evolved for a variety of equine pursuits.

Horses eat grass; in the wild state they lived on steppelands and developed flight as a principal weapon of defence. All the characteristics that a horse needs as a herd animal or an animal of flight are to be seen in most of its patterns of behaviour and requirements, and also its body structure.

Animal of Flight

Flight demands speed and demands possession of long, powerful legs and a slim body. But physical structure is not the only important criteria for speed, there is also the provision of air to organs and the regulation of temperature.

The nostrils of a horse are large and very flexible so as to permit maximum inhalation of air to the lungs. When moving at speed the horse does not build up heat, but, like man, sweats through the skin; the sweat then evaporates and allows the body to cool.

Biting and Kicking

Horses only bite and kick during their mutual power struggles to establish hierarchy, or as a defence in extreme emergencies if no flight is possible. Otherwise they are peaceable and only bite or kick as a result of wrong handling, as, for instance, if they are startled or, perhaps, irritated by the use of a very hard-bristled brush.

Animal of the Steppes

The steppes are covered to a certain extent in high grass. In order to have the widest possible angle of vision the horse has a long, highly-set neck that permits a much broader field of vision than, for example, human beings, as the eyes are placed at the side of the head. Also the ears are independent of each other and can 'move' to allow the horse to orientate itself from all directions at all times. The hoof of the horse is very hard and in the wild state the growth is worn back naturally. This is not so in domestication when the horse is shod and growth must be corrected by the farrier at regular intervals.

The mane and tail are used to keep away insects and the skin, which is highly sensitive, can be twitched for the same purpose.

The sense of smell is highly developed and very important. Every person has a unique smell, and sometimes, if only rarely, horses cannot stand the smell of their rider. Alternatively, they like the scent so much that they make this known with an expression of affection. The scent of human sweat evaporating from the skin due to fear will immediately be detected by the horse and the animal will display nervous behaviour as a result. Newly-painted fences are often suspect, not because of the bright colours but because of the smell.

Tactile hairs around the mouth and eyes act as sensors and should therefore not be removed for the sake of fashion.

In addition to all this the horse has an extremely acute sense of hearing, it is seven times more receptive than man to the difference in the frequency and intensity of sound waves. This should be remembered before shouting at a horse since the sound of a harsh voice is already a punishment in itself. Human footsteps will be heard and recognised by a horse from a long way off. The ability to differentiate sounds is so well developed

Tactile contact between individuals is an important part of communication.

that the horse in the stable will already recognise a sound precisely without having seen anything. These heightened senses especially facilitate the early sensing of danger, which man would only be aware of much later. Horses have 70 different senses and man has only five, and even these are often stunted or dulled. This knowledge should help us to understand that when horses shy or are reluctant to go forward it is because they may have sensed danger (real or imagined) that remains hidden to us. The early horse-peoples, from Scythians and Mongols to American Indians, understood and valued these highly developed senses, learning to rely on them as advance warnings of danger.

A Herd Animal

For the horse the herd represents a centre of security, with the individuals supporting each other. For example, foals and weak animals are placed in the middle of the herd and thus protected from danger. Members of the herd also keep guard and warn each other of danger: the animals never lie down all at the same time, not even in a stable – at least one will always keep watch. In order to live in company, there must be a hierarchy, and it is important for we humans to recognise it and appreciate its importance to the horse.

Within the herd the hierarchy is clearly delineated, with each animal having its place in the pecking order. When a new horse joins the herd, it will not be received with much enthusiasm initially until it has established its position in the hierarchy.

Quite often two or three horses will form a real friendship; they will graze close to each other, indulge in mutual grooming and call to each other when separated. Communication within the herd takes place through optical and acoustic signals such as face and ear signals, body posture and various sounds, and also through the sense of smell. These 'signals' are used for peaceable communication, for example an invitation to communal touching, in greeting, to play, to establish position, etc but they also serve to warn each other of the approach of possible enemies.

The most notable of the *optical signals* is the so-called danger posture. The head is raised, the ears are erect, muscles tense, tail lifted and the whole bodily expression is one of danger. All horses react appropriately to this and are immediately ready for flight. If one of them begins to gallop they will all go with it. A 'stampede' of horses is the ultimate example of the flight instinct, the panic spreading throughout the herd.

Ears

Movements of the *ears* and the *facial expression* are revealing of the state of mind. Erect ears denote alertness; a single ear flipped backwards can mean concentration on the rider, but can also indicate pain, particularly when both ears are turned back. Flaccid ears, hanging limply sideways, are usually a sign of drowsiness. ('Lop-eared' horses habitually carry the ears in this fashion as a result of a muscular malfunction. In horsy circles such horses are reputed to be very genuine and hard

A good roll on the grass is a natural requirement of all horses.

working, but there is no scientific explanation to support the assertion.)

Ears laid back flat to the head, with the white of the eyes showing and teeth bared are the signs of temper and aggression. Eyes are almost as revealing. In them one can discern contentment, fear and even the onset of sickness.

Whinnying, an acoustic signal, is exclusively a call or greeting sound. No horse whinnies out of fear of impending danger as the film makers would have us believe. When they are afraid, horses will snort by blowing air through their nostrils. In this way they test frightening objects or smells. Snorting has many meanings and, depending on the expression, it can also indicate contentment. If it is more like a deep sighing, then it is an expression of tenderness, as between mare and foal for example.

Squealing is sometimes heard when greeting or in play; some horses will squeal when bucking out of sheer high spirits.

Gentle nuzzling of the neck awakens memories of youth; every mare stimulates the neck of her foals.

Body Language

Whinnying	Happiness, Anticipation, Greeting.
Blowing/Snorting	Excited condition, greeting, locating strange objects.
Squealing	On making contact with other horses. High spirits or as a result of mare being in season.
Grunting sounds	When rolling or lying down.
Groaning	In pain.
Nodding the head	Agreement or preceding happiness on being fed.
Shaking the head	Displeasure.
Showing the teeth	Together with flattened ears, defence or attack.
Grinding the teeth	Displeasure.
Rolling the upper lip (upper lip turned up, head and neck upwards)	Sense a smell. Reaction to smells or unusual tastes.
Lower lip hanging loose	Dozing.
Ears erect	Attentiveness.
Ear play	Taking in the environment and sounds.
Ears pulled back	Taking in sounds from behind, or listening to the rider when one flicks back and forth.
Ears laid back	Temper, aggression, warning signal.
Stamping with front hoof	Displeasure, e.g. when being saddled.
Kicking forwards	Displeasure, resistance.
Scratching with hoof	Impatience.
Taking weight off rear foot	Resting.
Tail between legs	Tension, fear.
Swinging tail (when riding)	Loose, relaxed movement.
Swishing the tail	Displeasure, tension.
Rolling on the ground	Well-being, skin care; when connected with disquiet – threatened colic, pain.

The Needs of the Horse

Horses are creatures of habit and, to a degree, have to be accommodated in this respect. Otherwise, they exhibit a whole variety of natural actions when the environment allows them to do so. One of these is the so-called social skin care, or mutual grooming. To engage in this two horses will position themselves head to tail and groom each other in places they cannot reach themselves.

Rolling is fundamental in horses at liberty and a way of cleaning themselves. Horses roll in dust and mud because it is a pleasurable sensation but it also has the effect of removing dead hair and skin. As an additional bonus, rolling relaxes the back muscles and can relieve spinal problems in a quite natural way.

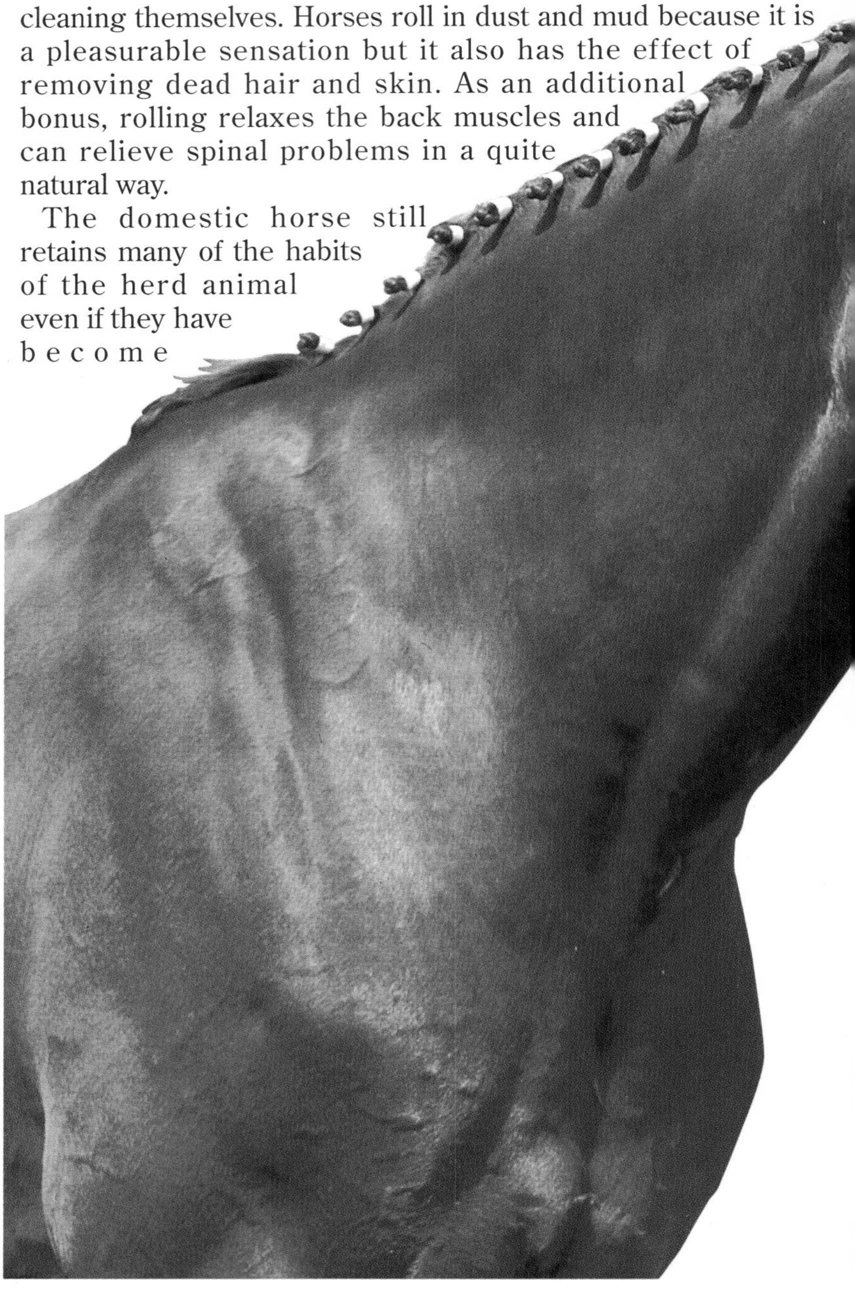

The domestic horse still retains many of the habits of the herd animal even if they have become

diluted by the dictates of domesticity. However, it is important that we realise the life deficiencies imposed by the domestic state.

Stables require to be light and airy if the horse is to be healthy.

Regular exercise for the stabled horse is another essential. The animal needs at least an hour-and-a-half, and usually more than that, each day. The horse may be given one rest day in the week but ideally some hours of it should be spent at freedom in the paddock. Indeed, all stabled horses benefit by being put out for a couple of hours a day. In autumn and winter clipped horses will require the protection of a waterproof, New Zealand-type rug.

It is necessary, also, to differentiate between exercise, which extends over a relatively protracted period and is carried out at slow paces, and *work* periods. The latter are short in duration but marked by high energy expenditure i.e. a session working in the school or over fences.

As a herd animal, horses do better when kept in the company of their own kind and, of course, they need to be fed in a manner as near to the natural feeding habit as possible.

At liberty, the horse eats continually, excreting waste products regularly once the stomach is two-thirds full. Obviously, this is not possible to duplicate in the case of the stabled animal. The best we can do, having regard to the horse's small stomach capacity, is to feed little and often, provide ample hay to provide roughage and ensure that fresh water is constantly available.

Routine is important to the horse and feed should be given at set times.

The quantity of energy-producing feed has always to correspond with the amount of energy-expending exercise. Too

Ideal conditions for horses; lush pasture, trees casting soft shady shadows for the herd to graze at leisure in the heat of the midday sun.

much food and too little exercise results in the horse misbehaving because he is 'over-fresh', and it will also cause the legs to fill with fluid and the general health to be affected.

A horse has a good long-term memory, but it cannot reason: if you are going to do something, then do it right away! Riders who wait until after dismounting before telling-off a horse for some 'mistake' are making a serious error. Immediate praise or reprimand is the best course of action. For a well-mannered horse it should be sufficient just to use a severe tone of voice as punishment, or to offer a titbit, or dismount and give a friendly pat as a reward!

The Horse

The four natural gaits of the horse are *walk, trot, canter* and *gallop*, the latter not being used in school work.

The sequence of footfalls when the WALK is begun with the movement of the left hindleg is: 1. Left hind, 2. Left fore; 3. Right hind; 4 Right fore. Four distinct and regular beats can be heard and should be felt by the rider.

The TROT is a two-beat gait, the horse bringing a diagonal pair of legs to the ground simultaneously (i.e. left fore and right hind or vice-versa). The footfall is then followed by a moment of suspension before the horse springs on the opposite diagonal to make the second beat in the gait.

The CANTER is a gait in three-time. If it begins with the engagement of the left hind, the sequence is: 1. Left hind; 2. Left diagonal (i.e. left fore and right hind touching the ground simultaneously) and 3. Right fore. The right foreleg is then termed the 'leading leg' and the horse is said to be on the 'right rein'. On circles to the right the horse leads with the right fore, whilst on the left circle the left fore is the leading leg. The horse is said to be on the 'wrong leg' or employing a 'false lead' when the opposite occurs.

(In advanced riding the balancing exercise of 'counter canter' is practised when the horse is asked to canter on just such a false lead.)

Usually the GALLOP is a four-beat gait and the sequence of footfalls in a four-beat gallop with the right fore leading is: 1. Left hind; 2. Right hind; 3. Left fore; 4. Right fore. There is then a moment of suspension when all four feet are in the air.

Modern dressage tests call for further sub-divisions in each gait.

MEDIUM WALK shows some extension with the hindfeet touching the ground in front of the prints of the forefeet.

COLLECTED WALK, obtained from the medium pace, comes from a shortening of the horse's base. In consequence the stride is shorter, more energetic and more elevated. The hindfeet then touch the ground *slightly behind* the imprint of the forefeet.

n Movement

EXTENDED WALK calls for a stretching forward of the head and neck and for the horse to cover as much ground as possible with each stride. However, there must still be regularity in the four, distinct footfalls, although again in this instance the hindfeet touch the ground in front of the imprint of the forefeet.

The same applies to FREE WALK, an extended pace which is one of rest performed with a long rein in minimal contact with the mouth.

The four TROT paces are WORKING, MEDIUM, COLLECTED and EXTENDED.

Working trot lies between medium and collected and inclines to the latter.

Medium lies between extended and collected and is more inclined to the former, the hindfeet touching down in the prints of the forefeet.

The canter pace is similarly divided and the same requirements are applied.

SPECIALIST GAITS. American breeds, like the American Saddle Horse, the Missouri Foxtrotter etc employ variations on the natural gaits. Harness racing horses and a number of European and Eastern breeds, also, employ the pacing gait when the legs are moved in lateral pairs rather than in the diagonal manner described for the trot gait.

(The REIN BACK is a movement, not a natural pace. The horse steps back in two-time using the legs in diagonal pairs. The steps are regular, distinct and made without hesitation.)

The Horse as a Teacher

Without doubt the older and well-trained riding horse is always the best teacher. But only a few riders have their first lessons on such a horse. Horses that habitually carry beginners and are given rough or incorrect aids become thick-skinned and less responsive. When beginning to learn, a quiet horse with easy paces will give the beginner a sense of safety and balance. It is helpful if the beginner rides the same horse for some time. Getting used to another horse is best done at a later stage when the rider is more confident and in better balance. All horses differ in movement, suppleness and temperament.

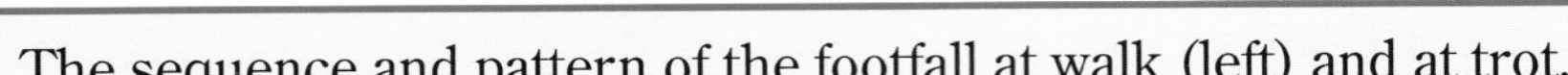

The sequence and pattern of the footfall at walk (left) and at trot.

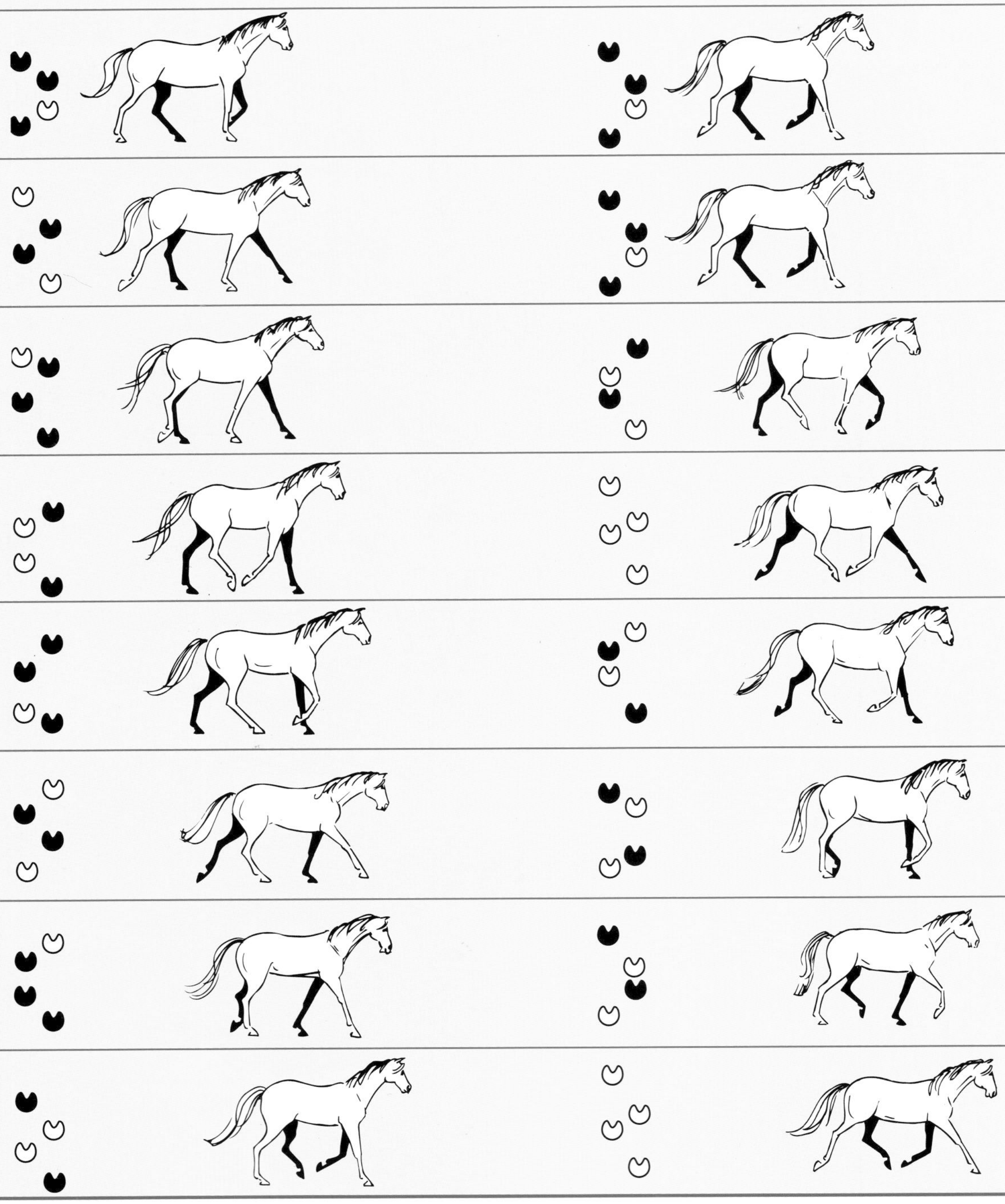

The sequence of movement in the canter – and gait with three distinct beats.	The overall outline and the placement of the limbs leading to the square halt.

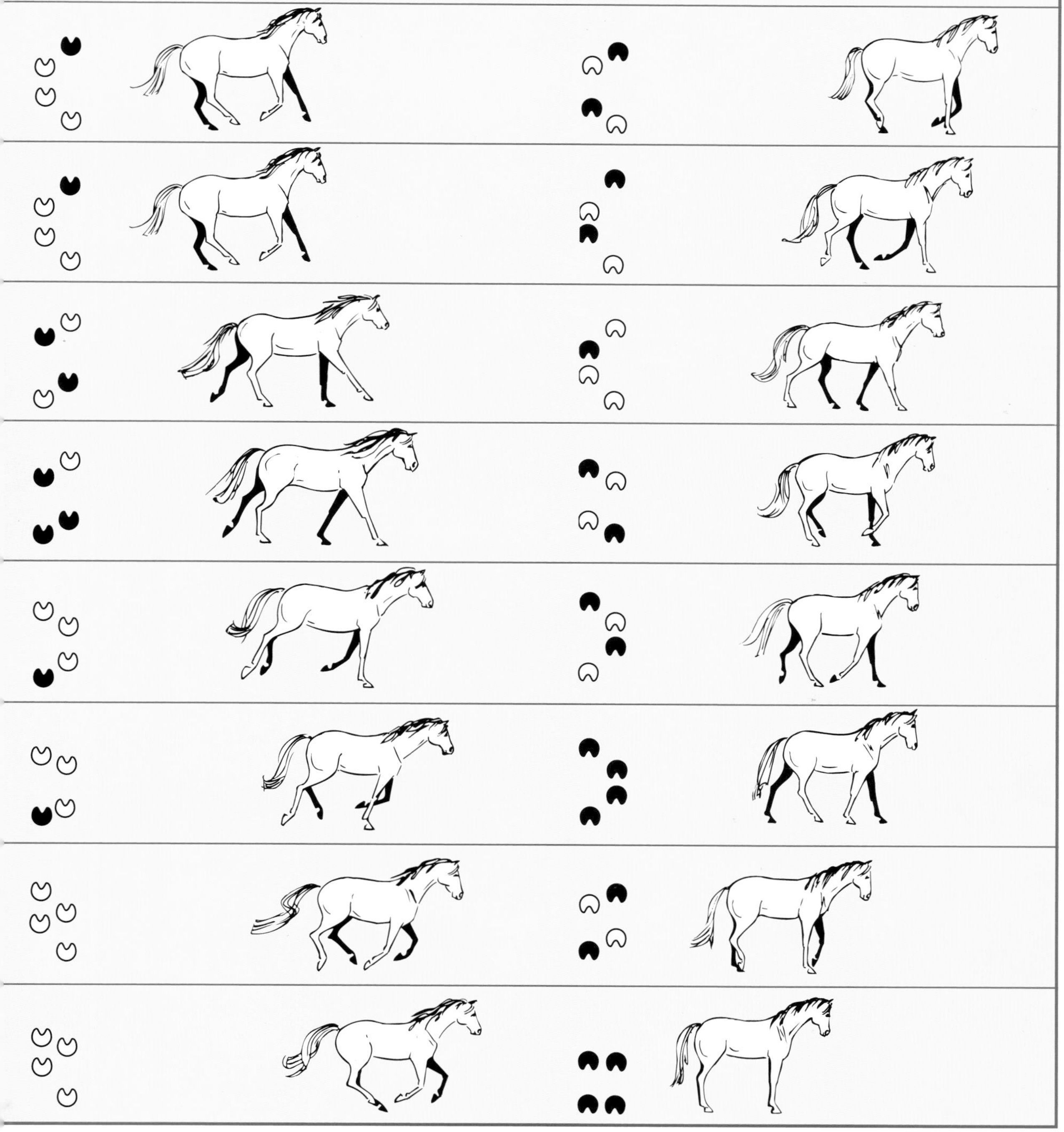

Equipment for Horse and Rider

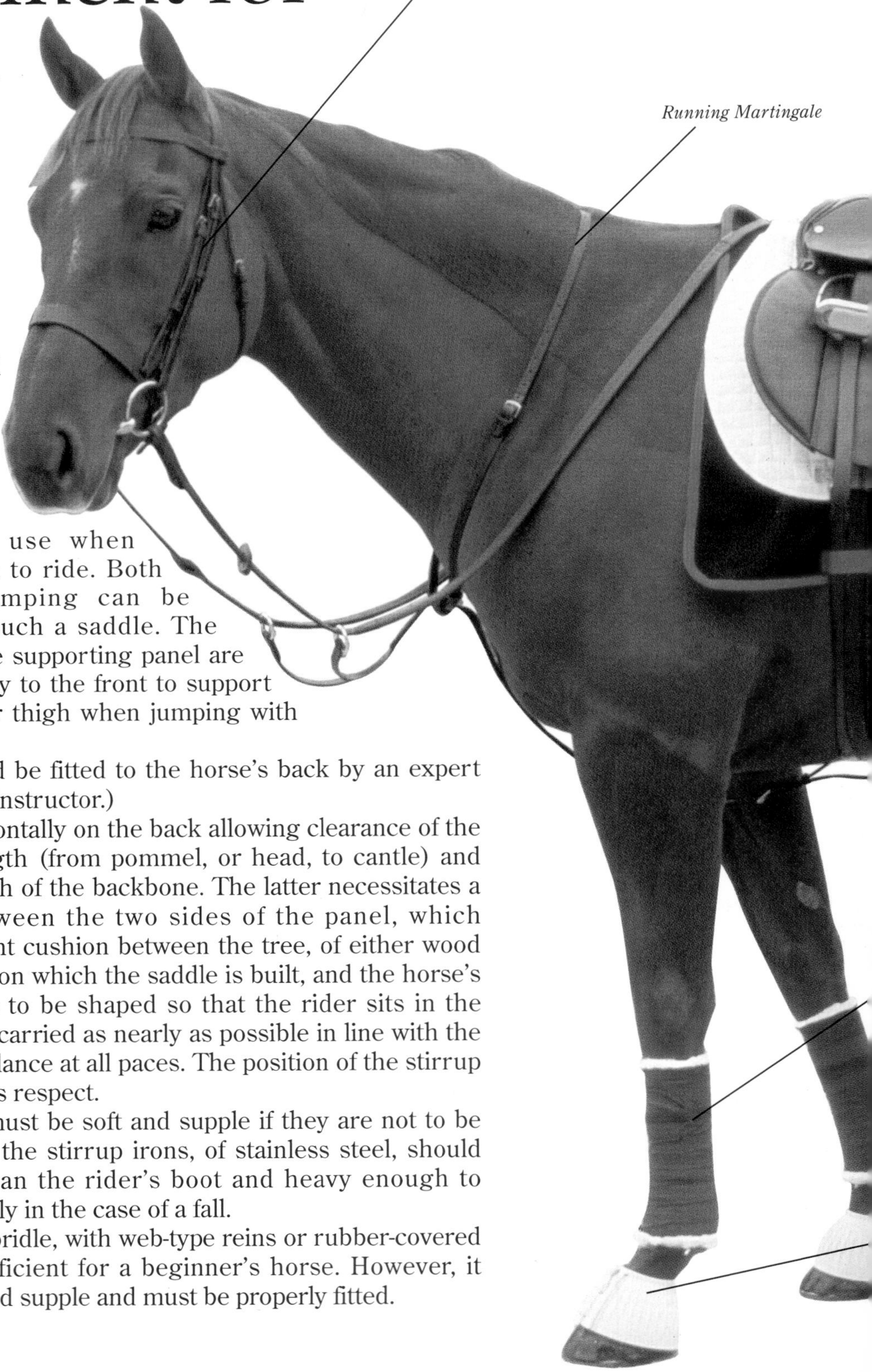

Snaffle bridle fitted with a plain cavesson noseband

Running Martingale

Equipment should be practical and simple but must be well-fitting. A general purpose saddle is the most suitable type to use when beginning to learn to ride. Both dressage and jumping can be undertaken with such a saddle. The saddle flaps and the supporting panel are extended sufficiently to the front to support the knee and upper thigh when jumping with shortened leathers.

The saddle should be fitted to the horse's back by an expert (not necessarily an instructor.)

It should lie horizontally on the back allowing clearance of the spine along its length (from pommel, or head, to cantle) and also across the width of the backbone. The latter necessitates a wide channel between the two sides of the panel, which represents a resilient cushion between the tree, of either wood or moulded plastic, on which the saddle is built, and the horse's back. The seat has to be shaped so that the rider sits in the deepest part and is carried as nearly as possible in line with the horse's centre of balance at all paces. The position of the stirrup bars is critical in this respect.

Stirrup leathers must be soft and supple if they are not to be uncomfortable and the stirrup irons, of stainless steel, should be a size larger than the rider's boot and heavy enough to release the foot easily in the case of a fall.

A simple, snaffle bridle, with web-type reins or rubber-covered ones is usually sufficient for a beginner's horse. However, it must be kept soft and supple and must be properly fitted.

General purpose saddle fitted over light, quilted saddle cloth

Quarter or exercise sheet for use in severe weather

ndages put on evenly over ad of Gamgee tissue

Brushing boots worn as a protection against blows from the opposite hoof. They are fastened with Velcro straps

Over-reach boots to protect he heels against a blow from hind foot.

Equipment for the Rider

The range of riding clothes etc is very wide.

For day-to-day riding jodhpurs, worn with a short leather jodhpur boot, or breeches worn with long leather or rubber riding boots, or indeed, half-chaps, are appropriate, but when riding casually there is no reason why jeans and a pair of full chaps should not be worn – so long as the boot is of a proper riding type with a good heel that prevents the foot slipping though the iron and becoming trapped.

Clothing above the waist depends on the occasion and the time of the year.

For hacking, hunting or jumping a hard hat of approved design is essential. For dressage, a hard hat is still a commonsense piece of equipment, but a top-hat has to be worn with the full dressage uniform of tail-coat etc which is obligatory in the more advanced competitions.

Riding whips, of the dressage type (about 1m in length) are useful schooling aids that can support the action of the leg. For jumping or cross-country a shorter whip is carried.

Preparation

The Riding Teacher

It is always advisable to go to a qualified instructor who will teach a recognised progression and observe the rules of safety. Additionally, the qualified teacher will be adequately insured against accidents that may happen to pupils under his care, although the current pre-occupation with law suits, often over trivialities, is not a trend to be encouraged. In the present climate there are all too many self-appointed experts teaching without recognised qualifications or, indeed, much relevant experience.

Most of them claim, with minimal justification, to teach to one, true 'classical' seat – a few may do so but many more are 'false prophets' that do more harm than good. They are to be avoided.

It is an advantage if the riding instructor, as well as being a gifted teacher, is also a good rider and can demonstrate this, thus providing a good role model for his pupils.

Methods of teaching riding are continually improving, so the instructor always needs to be open to new ideas and to keep himself up to date. It goes without saying, that the instructor will need to be something of a psychologist in dealing with both horses and riders and have an innate ability to match the rider with a compatible mount.

Instructions must always be clear and precise and the instructor should stress the importance of carrying them out accurately. Positive correction and instruction, such as when nipping mistakes in the bud, are accepted by riders anxious to learn and should not be resented.

All correction will, however, be useless if the rider himself does not exercise self-discipline, seek to improve

for Riding

mental consciousness and the physical requirements needed for riding.

A good riding instructor will also give theoretical lessons. The rider will only be able to put any correction into practice if he has grasped theoretically what he must work for. Afterwards only slight correction will be necessary. Without theoretical knowledge it will not be possible to attain the desired goals.

In the theoretical lessons the riding instructor will address all the pupils' questions that they were not able to answer during the riding lesson itself.

Horse and rider must build up a relationship of trust with the instructor.

Preparing for the Riding Lesson

A good riding lesson begins with the horse in the stable, when sufficient time has to be taken to prepare the horse for the

If a rider can become 'one of the herd', then it will be much easier to gain the respect of all those horses.

riding lesson. A quiet, properly carried out preparation of the horse is particularly necessary for successful training sessions at every level. Knowing how to handle the horse before and after the lesson and acquiring a basic knowledge of horse care is part of the whole process of learning to ride. Riding lessons on their own do not make a rider.

This theoretical and practical instruction is necessary in order to obtain certain skills in handling horses. To be able to lead a horse correctly is just as important as the proper use of aids. The basis of trust between horse and rider is built up in handling the horse before and after the lesson. Quiet and composed steps should be taken towards the stable, the rider carrying the headcollar and lead rein then, under proper instruction, the horse can be groomed and saddled. Call the horse by its name and approach it slowly but with confidence. Then stand up to the shoulder and stroke the neck. The headcollar, held initially in the left hand, can be slipped on carefully from below using both hands. The horse should then be tied to a tethering ring using a quick-release knot. To be recognised as a member of the herd is a prerequisite of handling horses. If man (rider or instructor) is accepted in the same light as dominant mare or leading stallion, then the position has been secured.

Before the lesson the horse is prepared carefully, particular attention being given to the fitting of the equipment.

It is very important that the rider should earn the trust and affection of the horse, which is best done by spending time with the animal, handling him and talking quietly. Although the horse does not understand our language it is sensitive enough to recognise the tone of voice immediately and can gain confidence from it.

Nervousness, haste, fear, loud shouting only disturb horses, as do sudden and hasty movements and wild gestures. So, speak quietly and make only deliberate movements, and remember that horses can appreciate and respond to physical contact.

Don't approach a horse suddenly from behind. Speak quietly so that it is aware of your presence, otherwise it could become frightened and then act instinctively by kicking out. When approaching a horse, speak to it and stand up close before offering an outstretched open hand for it to smell. Titbits should also be offered on the flat of the hand so that the horse does not bite the fingertips by mistake!

A headcollar and lead rein are always required to lead a horse. As a rule the horse is led from the left with the leader holding the lead with the right hand some few inches from the headcollar. The end of the lead, after it has been passed across the body should be held in the left hand.

If the horse is bridled, then both reins should be passed over the head and held in the same manner as the lead rein. Lead the horse from a position at the shoulder, encouraging him to walk forward, if necessary, by tapping him upon the flank with a whip held in the left hand and passed behind the back.

When releasing a horse in the paddock take him through the gateway and into the field. Turn him to face you before removing the headcollar so that his hind legs are well out of the way should he kick out in excitement. It is not advisable to try to catch up one horse from a group, it will always be reluctant to leave its herd companions. Instead bring up two or three at once if it is at all possible.

The tail should be brushed out regularly and the tangles removed.

Always tie up a horse with a headcollar fitted with a rope, never, ever by the bridle, which could be broken and even cause injury if the horse was to pull back in panic. Horses should never be tied to movable or insecure objects such as door handles, box doors, loose fence stakes, not even for a minute or two. If at all possible, a horse that is tied up should not be left on its own. When tethering use a rope fitted with a panic hook at one end and use a quick-release knot at the other. It also makes good sense to use a leather headcollar rather than the colourful nylon ones as a broken headcollar is, after all, preferable to an injured horse.

As a general rule headcollars should not be worn in the field lest they get caught up in a hedge, fencing or gate fastening.

Picking up Feet

This should be done by standing facing towards the tail next to the appropriate leg. With the hand stroke from the shoulder or croup, first going along the outside then the inside of the leg, right down to the fetlock and then say 'up' whilst lifting the leg and taking it a little forward. Horses quickly understand the combination of hand and voice and will virtually lift the leg on command.

If the foot is to stay lifted for some time, then the fetlock can be rested on the upper thigh.

The feet are cleaned out with a hoof-pick being drawn either side of the frog from rear to front.

Care of a Grass-kept Horse

Horses that spend time in a field or paddock do not need to be groomed in the same way as a stabled horse, it is sufficient to brush off the surface mud. More thorough brushing than this would remove the protective grease from the skin. When coats are changing the loose hair can, of course, be brushed out. Leg hair and the mane and tail can be brushed clean but need not be thinned as they give protection against the weather and, in summer, the flies.

Care of a Stabled Horse

Stabled horses need to be groomed daily to keep the coat and skin clean. Waste matter, which increases as a result of consuming quantities of artificial foods, is disposed of through an increased breathing rate, normal excrement *and* through the skin itself. Grooming, as opposed to the 'lick and a promise' given before exercise is best done *after* the horse has worked when he is warm and the skin pores are open. Strapping, wisping vigorously with a coiled rope of damp hay, or hand massaging are best left to the end of the day to encourage circulation during the night hours when the blood flow will naturally slow down.

Grooming

The first thing to do is to pick out the feet catching the dirt removed in a stable skip. Feet should not be washed too

Horses can come to appreciate a cooling shower but, for safety's sake, the practice should be introduced very gradually.

frequently as the water tends to remove the natural oil secreted from the coronary band. The feet can, however, be oiled regularly both to assist nature and to improve the appearance.

The body of the horse is cleaned with a soft, body brush, not a stiff-bristled dandy-brush, the purpose of which is to remove mud from unclipped areas of the legs. The brush itself is cleaned after every two or three strokes with a metal curry-comb, which is *never* used on the horse. (Rubber/plastic combs may be used on the body for the massaging effect and to remove loose hair.)

Grooming starts high up on the neck, behind the ears, the brush being applied from front to rear and with one's full weight behind the stroke.

The head is cleaned separately with the body brush, which in this area is used very gently and with care being taken not to bang the bony projections with the corners of the wooden back. It is finished off with a soft cloth.

Mane and tail are brushed out lock by lock with the soft brush (not a dandy-brush which would break the hairs) and then are 'laid' with a damp water brush.

The dock, eyes and nose, are cleaned with separate sponges.

Geldings will need to have the sheath washed out periodically and this is best done wearing a domestic rubber glove and using a thin sponge dipped in warm water.

Manes and tails can be washed at intervals to remove accumulations of grease and, for the sake of appearance, most owners trim the mane and tail by 'pulling' the surplus hairs.

Initially, the mane can be thinned with the mane comb, and then the long hairs pulled out from the *underside* of the mane. If hair is pulled out from the top the mane will grow upright and spikey. The length of the mane is best determined by the use of a sharp pen-knife against the thumb. Never use scissors; they will give a wholly unprofessional 'step' effect.

Those hairs that stick out sideways on the tail are either pulled out sideways (like the mane) or cut level. To do this use curved scissors so as not to injure the horse. Afterwards the dock of the tail should be greased so that the stubble does not tickle. The tail can also be cut to the correct length. First the tail is thoroughly brushed out, then hold all the hairs together from the root of the tail and run the hand downwards to the end, now cut the end of the hairs diagonally towards the horse, level with the hock joint. The angle of the cut will be balanced by the position of the tail when moving.

Horses can be washed using an animal shampoo if the coat has become very dirty or if it has become sweated at exercise. However, the animal must be dried off thoroughly with particular attention paid to the heels. Hosing the lower legs helps prevent swelling and is enjoyed by most horses. Just how playful you can be with a hose elsewhere on the body depends upon the individual and it is as well to assess the reaction before becoming too adventurous. Very few horses appreciate a 'water fight'.

Grooming, strapping and generally handling the horse at close quarters provides the best possible basis for creating a trusting, understanding relationship between horse and rider.

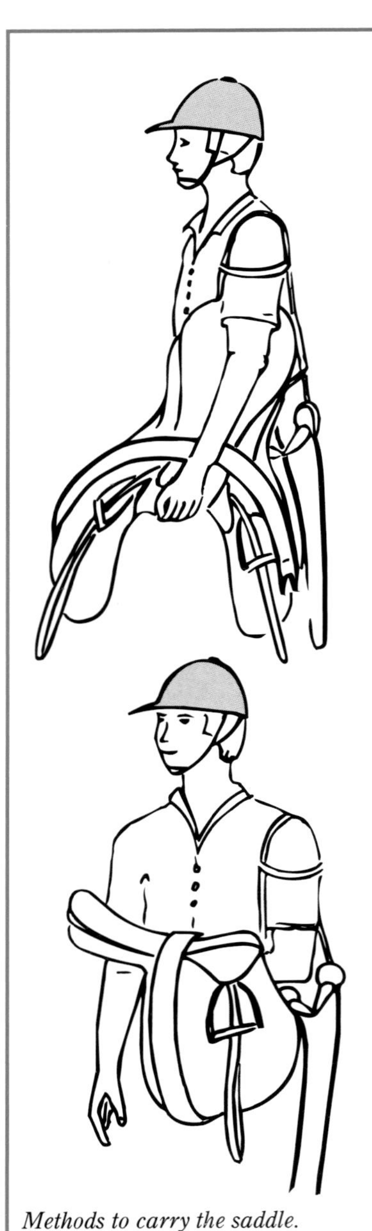
Methods to carry the saddle.

Putting on a Saddle

The saddle is placed on the horse from the left-hand side with the stirrups pulled up and the girth folded over. It is positioned carefully behind the withers on the back of the horse and then gently pushed backwards. The saddle cloth or light numnah should be pulled up into the gullet so that it does not lie on the withers. The girth, made of leather or padded cotton material, should be adjusted just tightly enough to prevent the saddle slipping. It can be fastened a hole or two tighter when the rider is on board. Most horses (nearly all horses) will blow themselves out when the saddle is first girthed up and for this reason, as well as for the animal's comfort the girth is best adjusted in the suggested stages.

The Bridle

For schooling, jumping and cross-country a simple snaffle bridle, with a plain cavesson, a drop- or crossover noseband, is usually sufficient. However, strong-pulling horses may need additional restraints. Double bridles are, of course, used in advanced dressage competitions – a case of a bridle for the educated rider and the educated horse.

Drop- or crossover nosebands by fastening under the bit keep the mouth closed and so prevent the horse evading the action of the bit by sliding it to one side or other of the mouth. They will also increase the rider's control by causing the head to be lowered and the nose retracted in response to the rein action.

There are very many types of snaffle bit, but whichever is chosen it is better to use one with a thick, soft mouthpiece that will spread the pressure over a greater area of sensory nerves. Narrow mouthpieces can be sharp and sometimes very severe. Frequently they provoke the very resistance that they are thought to prevent, and may even cause the horse to attempt to run away in its efforts to escape the discomfort imposed on the mouth.

The fitting of the bridle is of great importance since it affects materially the horse's relationship with the rider under saddle, a matter that will be reflected in the animal's behaviour and way of going.

A bridle that causes discomfort, because of the way it is fitted to the head, encourages resistance and makes harmonious horsemanship impossible.

The size of the bit and its position in the mouth is critical. The butt ends of the mouthpiece should project no more than a half-inch on either side of the mouth. The bit itself should be sufficiently high to cause the corners of the lips to wrinkle in 'a smile'. Many bits are fitted too low in the mouth and cause discomfort by coming up against the incisor teeth. That situation is an encouragement for the horse to put his tongue over the top of the mouthpiece and evade the action altogether.

Otherwise, major sources of trouble are the browband and the throatlatch. If the former is too short, and therefore too tight, it pulls the headpiece against the back of the ears. Horses will often react to the irritation on the sensitive area by shaking the head, sometimes quite violently. There is then a real danger of the head-shaking becoming habitual, the horse persisting even when the browband has been changed for a larger one. As a guide, allow for the insertion of one finger between the browband and the forehead and, just as importantly, ensure that the browband is positioned 25mm (1 inch) lower than the base of the ears.

A throatlatch adjusted too tightly is not only very uncomfortable but can restrict the breathing and will certainly prevent the horse from flexing at the poll. Allow for three fingers to be inserted between it and the horse's gullet.

Obviously, the two cheekpieces must be adjusted to an equal length. It is usual for their buckles to be in line with, or just below, the eye with the buckle fastening the headpiece of the noseband similarly positioned.

When a plain cavesson noseband (from *caveçon*, meaning halter) is used, the manuals recommend that the fitting should allow for the insertion of two fingers between it and the head. The origin of the instruction are the old cavalry manuals which made the ruling for the sake of cosmetic uniformity.

A noseband of this type is more effective when it is lowered a hole or two and fastened snugly round the jaw (above the bit, of course) so as to ensure at least a partial closing of the mouth.

A drop noseband, when the rear strap fastens under the bit to effect a far more positive closure of the mouth, is more complex and its fitting demands commensurately more care.

The nosepiece should be fitted 6.5-7.5cm (2½-3 inches) *above* the nostril at the end of the nasal bone, adjusted lower than that it will cause unacceptable interference with the breathing. In fact, the position of the nosepiece is dependent upon the rear strap being of sufficient length. If it is too short the nosepiece will, inevitably, lie so low as to obstruct the nasal passages.

The forms of cross nosebands, like the Flash and the Grakle, or Fig.8, need careful fitting but are probably less potentially severe than the conventional drop noseband.

The most sophisticated bitting arrangement is the double bridle and its fitting, in the instance of the novice rider, should be under the supervision of the instructor.

In the double bridle the curb bit lies in the mouth below the snaffle, the latter usually being referred to as the bradoon (or bridoon) after the classical French terminology.

The snaffle must still correspond to the size of the mouth, but the curb has to fit *exactly.* It should be as close to the outside of the lips as possible without actually pressing on them. If it is too big, as so many are, it can easily be displaced to one side or other of the mouth and the action impaired in consequence. Moreover, since it will irritate the horse we disturb the concentration and disrupt the harmony of the performance.

The best rule of all for the positioning of the curb bit in the mouth is this "*place the mouthpiece on that part of the bars exactly opposite the chin groove*". (The bars are the area of gum between the molar and incisor teeth.)

The adjustment of the curb chain is made by tilting the bit so that the chain is brought into play when the cheek (of the bit) reaches a 45 degree angle. The curb chain, with the links lying flat, is kept in position by the lip-strap connecting the two bit cheeks.

The pressures exerted on tongue and bars varies according to the size and shape of the port, the raised curve in the centre of the mouthpiece. A shallow port places more emphasis on the tongue and less on the bars. A deeper one, allowing more room for the tongue, increases the potential for pressure on the bars of the mouth.

Putting on the Bridle

Before putting on the bridle it must be arranged properly with the throatlatch and noseband unbuckled. The headcollar is taken off and the reins placed over the head and neck of the horse. Standing at the nearside shoulder, facing the front, the rider's right hand holds the bridle in the centre of the headpiece and guides it upwards on the horse's nose from below. The middle finger and thumb of the left hand are inserted between the lips of the horse, to open the mouth and guide the bit gently into the mouth. Meanwhile, the right hand takes the bridle upwards to a position where it can be slipped over first one ear and then the other. Then the buckles of throatlatch and noseband can be fastened.

DOUBLE BRIDLE

1. *Headpiece*
2. *Bradoon Sliphead*
3. *Cavesson Headpiece*
4. *Keeper for point of headpiece*
5. *Billet with hook-stud fastening, bradoon rein*
6. *Fly Link*
7. *Curb Rein*
8. *Lipstrap*
9. *Curb Chain*
10. *Port*
11. *Curb Ring*
12. *Dee Loop for lipstrap*
13. *Curb Hook*
14. *Bradoon*
15. *Cavesson Nosepiece*
16. *Cavesson Cheekpiece*
17. *Throatlatch*
18. *Browband*

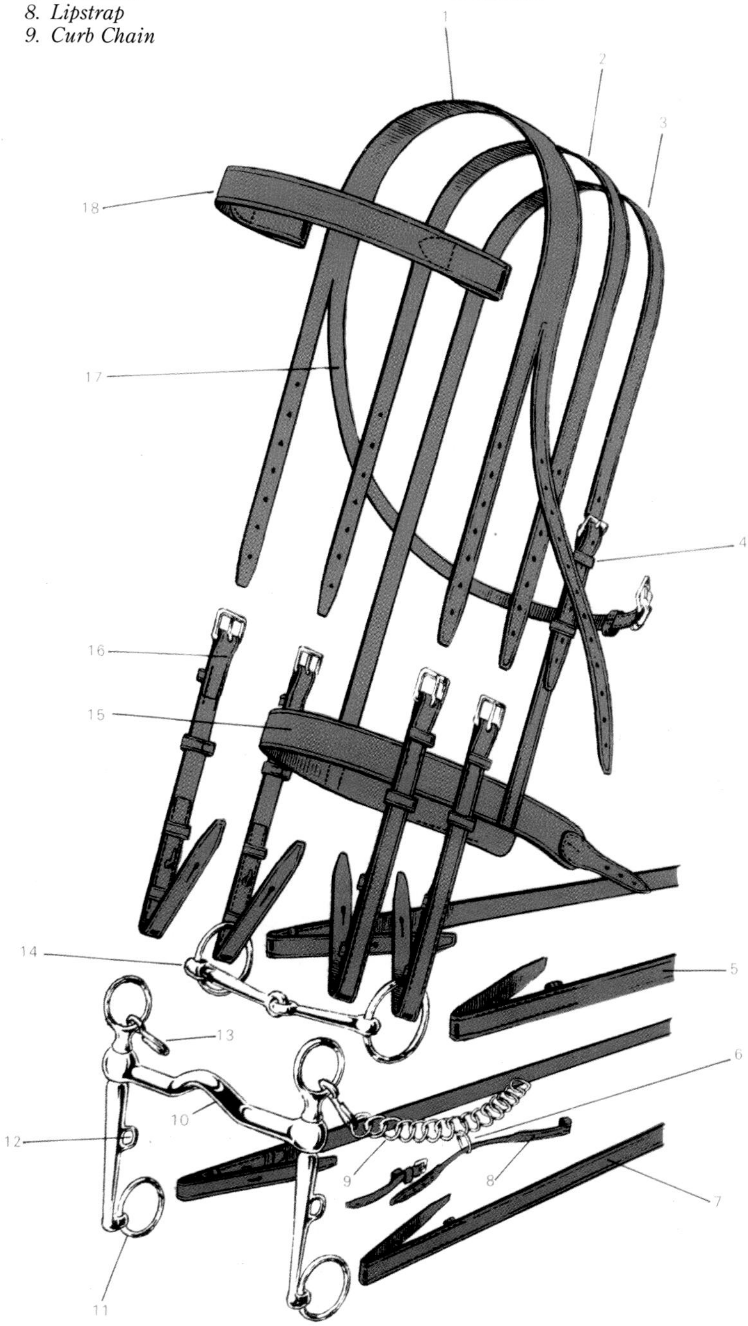

Boots and Bandages

Boots and bandages are employed to protect the legs from injuries which might be caused by a foot striking into the leg, and/or to give support to tendons and ligaments. Bandages are, of course, also used in the application of veterinary dressings etc.

Bandages are *always* applied over a pad of felt, Gamgee tissue or similar material so as to ensure equal pressure throughout the length. They are wound on evenly from top to bottom and any knot involved should be on the outside of the limb, not on the front of the bone where it would interfere with circulation.

However, bandaging is an art acquired only with much practice. In most instances, gaiters, now made in great variety from hi-tech materials, are probably more efficient and are certainly more easily fitted.

As a precaution, it is advisable for horses to wear boots when schooling. Older horses will also benefit from the support given by boots and young ones, especially when worked on the lunge, should always have the protection afforded by carefully chosen boots covering the lower limbs. It should be remembered that young horses, like young children, lack co-ordination and in the case of the former are very likely to strike into themselves when moving in circles.

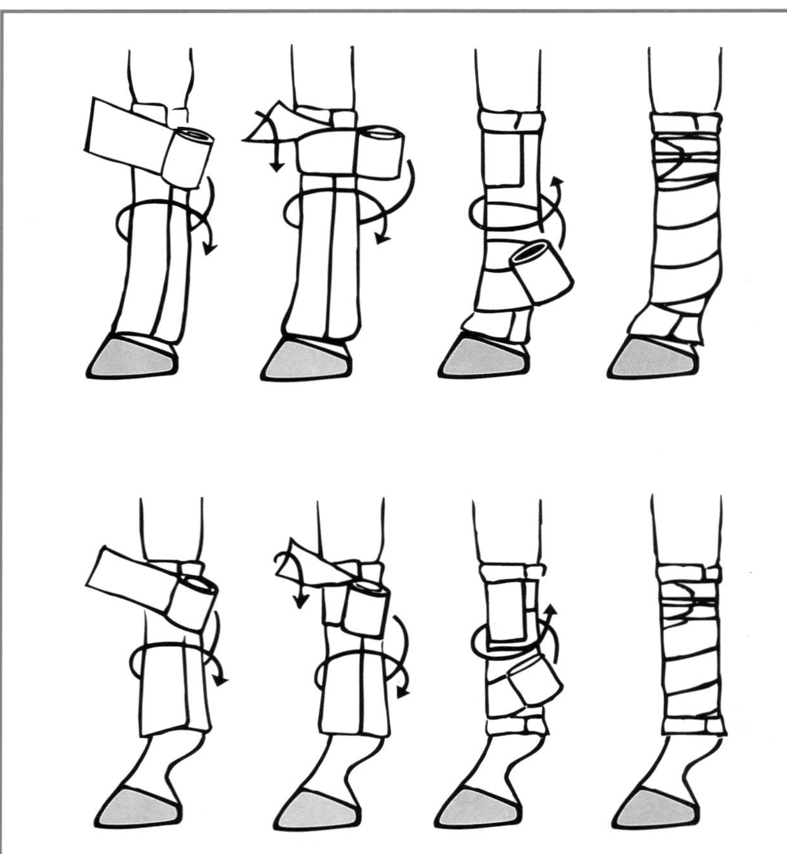

The art of bandaging is one that must be learnt by observation and long practise. It is essential to ensure equal tension from top to bottom.

Hosing the legs prevents swelling

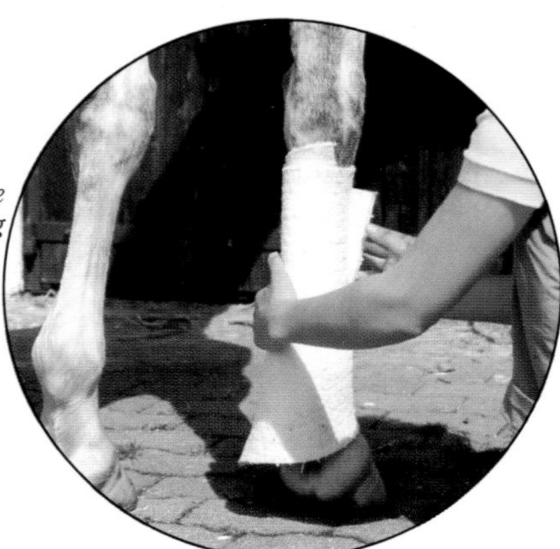

Putting the pads in place preparatory to bandaging

Bandaging over the felt pad

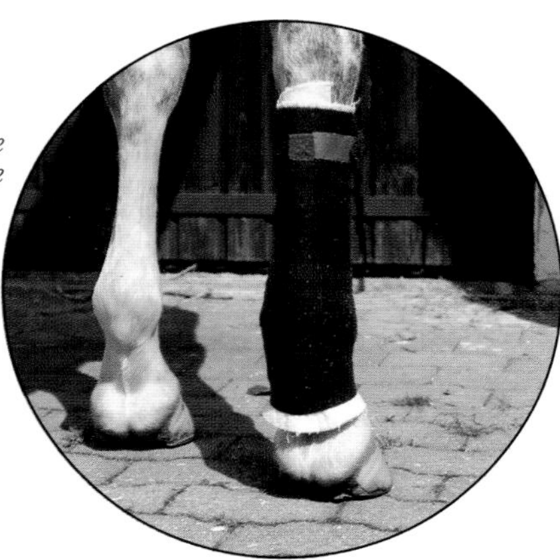

The completed stable bandage

Sponging the eyes

Pad to prevent pressure on the withers

Washing the tail

Rug turned neatly back under the surcingle

After the Lesson

At the end of every lesson the rider must make a conscious effort to be in sympathy with the horse. We have to reinforce the *rapport* and this is more easily attainable if the lesson ends on a good note. If a horse is having difficulty with a movement or some aspect of the training, go back to something that he enjoys and can do well. The lesson will then end with a contented rider transmitting his pleasure to the horse *and* with a horse happy in the knowledge that he has pleased his partner.

Nothing is so damaging to the principle of harmony as a discontented rider ending the lesson with feelings of anger, annoyance and frustration.

When the ride is over it is important to sponge the horse down, cover it and gently dry its legs.

Learning on the Lunge

Any meaningful riding course begins with at least 10 hours on the lunge. Experienced riders know that training on the lunge never comes to an end if the horse and rider are to harmonise with each other ever more finely. Beginner or advanced riders on the lunge can concentrate completely on their own bodies. In a relaxed physical state, helped by closing the eyes, it is possible to *absorb* the movements of the horse and to acquire a greater consciousness of one's balance. Breathing exercises are established in the first lunge lesson and should never be neglected, as breathing properly means living properly. Actors, speakers, dancers and singers, for example, know that their art begins with breathing. Swimmers, sprinters, golfers – all must first learn to breathe correctly in order to improve their performance.

In all the different paces and transitions, the rider must learn to allow his body to conform with the balance of the horse. In the end, he should be able to do so quite independently of hand and reins. Only when this has been achieved can the reins be taken in the hand. If this is done too soon then the rider will automatically hold the reins tightly and never really learn to sit properly loosened. A common mistake is to let a rider ride on his own too early. Because such riders lack balance, are not relaxed, and lack trust in the horse, they continually hold tightly with hands and legs, which is the instinctive behaviour of human beings – thus insecurity causes a clinging effect that inhibits the balance and movement of the horse and detracts irrevocably from the essential mental *rapport*.

Nonetheless, the rider's confidence, and therefore relaxation, will be helped by the provision of a neckstrap which can be held lightly in the fingers of the outside hand (i.e. right hand on the circle left and vice-versa).

Once the rider is sitting comfortably without stirrups and with the legs hanging naturally down the sides of the horse, the instructor can begin the BREATHING exercises which are the foundation for the work on the lunge.

The rider should be asked to take three deep breaths, and in doing this emphasis should be placed on BREATHING OUT. All the air should be expelled until the rider is deeply and completely relaxed, sitting in an almost collapsed position. In breathing out he should imagine that all the fear and tension of the body flows out with the breath. On breathing in he straightens up like a flower unfolding, quite slowly and anticipating something happy occurring. The rider must learn to breathe consciously and strengthen his regular breathing with appropriate mental pictures relative to these descriptions. When breathing consciously, we can always and everywhere in moments of stress, anger or fear return to these three deep breaths and begin to feel better again right away.

Only when riders can breathe regularly and literally breathe out the first few moments of tension are they ready to move on to something new. Riders should not be pressed into a mould when sitting on the horse, but should feel themselves into their own body consciousness and be aware when they are sitting straight and balanced on the horse. With eyes closed they should consciously absorb this feeling of balance. One or two easy exercises can be performed whilst standing still, such as: circling the arms, turning the head and arms without moving the pelvis, stretching both arms upwards without taking the weight off the buttocks, hanging the arms down loosely at the same time circling the shoulders backwards and forwards, shrugging the shoulders, doing everything with the hands and arms loose. These are the foundations for all body consciousness. Only in this way can the beginner arrive at natural movement and co-ordination relatively quickly.

If the riding instructor now begins to lead the horse at walk, quietly and evenly, then the rider will build up, for the first time, a relationship with the horse and the instructor.

Further breathing exercises should follow whilst walking, as before. As the horse moves slowly around the circle on the lunge the riding instructor can gradually and carefully allow the horse to begin a gentle trot. The rider in breathing out remains in the deep seat without slumping, but allows the movement of the trot to swing through the whole body. This is only possible if the body of the rider permits it and allows the movement of the horse to pull them deep into the saddle. In this way the rider learns how to sit from the start. An experienced riding instructor and a horse with soft, easy paces are naturally prerequisites.

The instructor may even allow the rider to experience the movement of the canter in the first lunge lesson. With just a little encouragement a good lunge horse can be brought to canter and the rider, breathing evenly and sitting a little behind the vertical, allowing the lift of the canter to go through loosened hips, will experience a wonderful feel of the pace.

The three kinds of pace are demonstrated only briefly to the rider. The amount of time is not important, only the first experience of the feel of the movement in the three basic paces. The horse can be brought back to the walk and then to halt and during a pause the tension can be removed from the rider that cannot be dispersed whilst moving. As a result of these pauses, along with directed breathing exercises with the rider, the horse too will loosen up and become more comfortable for the beginner to sit on. This first lesson on the lunge lays the foundation stone for all that is to follow in basic training. That which impresses itself upon the rider as feeling correct and very easy will remain stored in the brain and become an instinctive feeling. A feeling for movement cannot be learnt. ONLY in a loosened body without blocks of any kind can these movement patterns be stored and then they will always return. Theoretical explanations are essential as the rider must first understand the relationships and sequences of the movement with the mind. When the rider then gets on the horse they should only feel how it moves under them.

The vaulting discipline on the trained lunge horse exemplifies the ideal of suppleness and harmonious body control.

Beginning to Ride

Mounting and Dismounting

Before mounting, the rider stands on the left-hand side of the horse with the back to the head of the horse. The rider takes the reins in the left hand and establishes a light contact with the horse's mouth; as a result the horse can no longer move forwards. The left rein should be held a little shorter than the right to prevent the horse turning outwards. The left hand now grasps the mane or the front of the saddle, the left foot is placed in the stirrup, which is turned forwards in a clockwise direction, and the right hand grasps either the centre of the saddle or the saddle edge. The rider then pushes himself up with the right foot, swings the right leg over the croup of the horse and slides carefully into the saddle. The right foot is then placed into the right-hand stirrup from the outside.

When dismounting, the rider maintains contact with the mouth of the horse and the reins are held in the left hand, which rests on the crest of the mane. Both feet are taken out of the stirrups, the right leg is swung over the croup, and the rider lets himself slide down more or less with some swing away from the body of the horse.

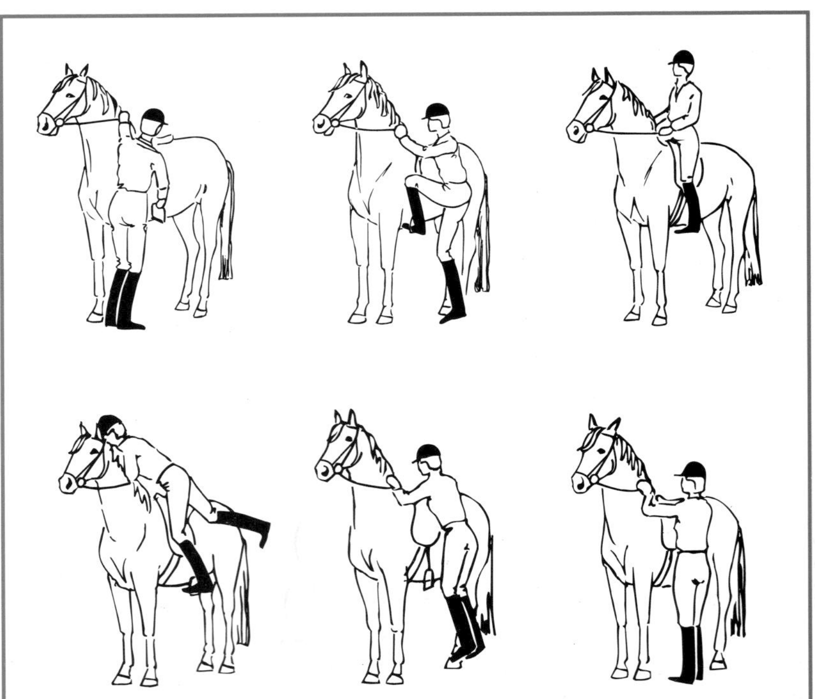

Mounting – take a full breath at each stage. Dismounting – after landing keep a hand on the rein.

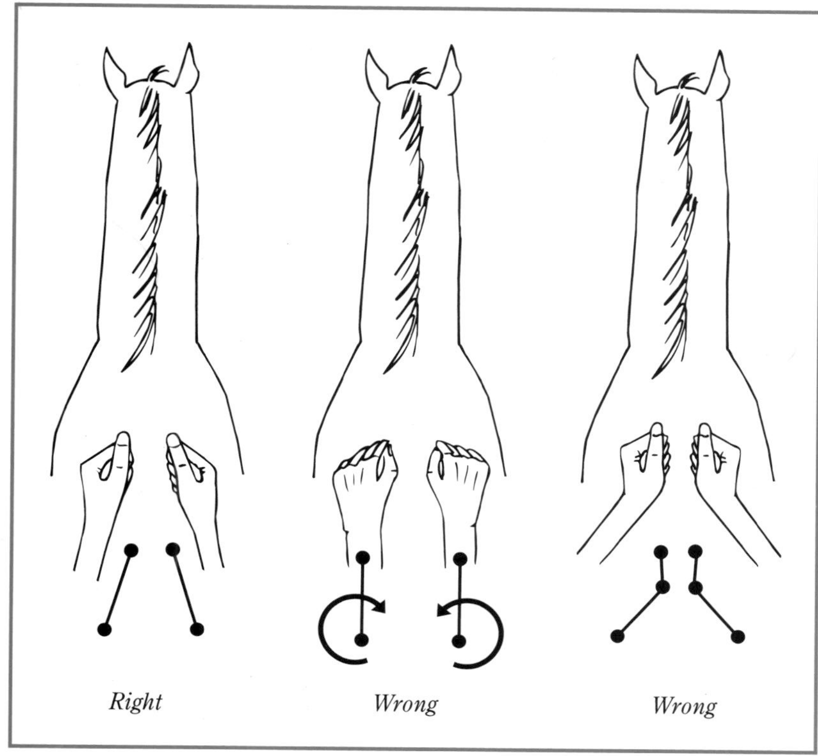

Taking up the Reins

After mounting, the reins are taken up and a contact with the mouth of the horse is then established. Both hands take up the reins from above, holding them between ring and little finger, through a lightly closed hand over the forefinger. The thumb is placed lightly on top and the ends of the reins hang to the right. A well-ridden horse naturally transmits a feeling of submission when the reins are taken up, more so than a riding school horse that is continually being ridden by beginners and may be defensive and less responsive in the mouth. From the beginning the learner should take care to keep his hand upright, i.e. the small fingers are nearer to each other than the thumbs, and the inside of the nails should be just visible.

It is also essential from the very beginning to create an even contact with the horse's mouth: a feeling similar to holding an elastic band should be a conscious aim.

Seat at Walk

Before mounting, the stirrups can only be adjusted approximately. A length according to the measurements of the arm can be used as a very rough guide: the fingertips are placed at the buckle of the stirrup leather and with hand outstretched the stirrup iron is lifted to the armpit.

Before mounting, the rider consciously takes three deep breaths, as described in the sitting exercises, and at the same time thinks of relaxing on breathing out – breathing in calmness – repeating this three times. Every horse will stand quietly if the rider carries out all the procedures without hurrying.

In the sitting exercises the rider has learned to let the legs hang loose and long and to maintain a balance on both buttocks. Nothing changes from this basic position when the stirrup is taken up as described. The rider will, with well-developed body consciousness, feel the length of stirrup that is most comfortable.

As in the sitting exercises on the lunge horse, three deep breaths should be taken on halting the horse – breathing out and remaining deep and heavy in the saddle – breathing in and sitting erect like an opened flower, but keeping the buttocks

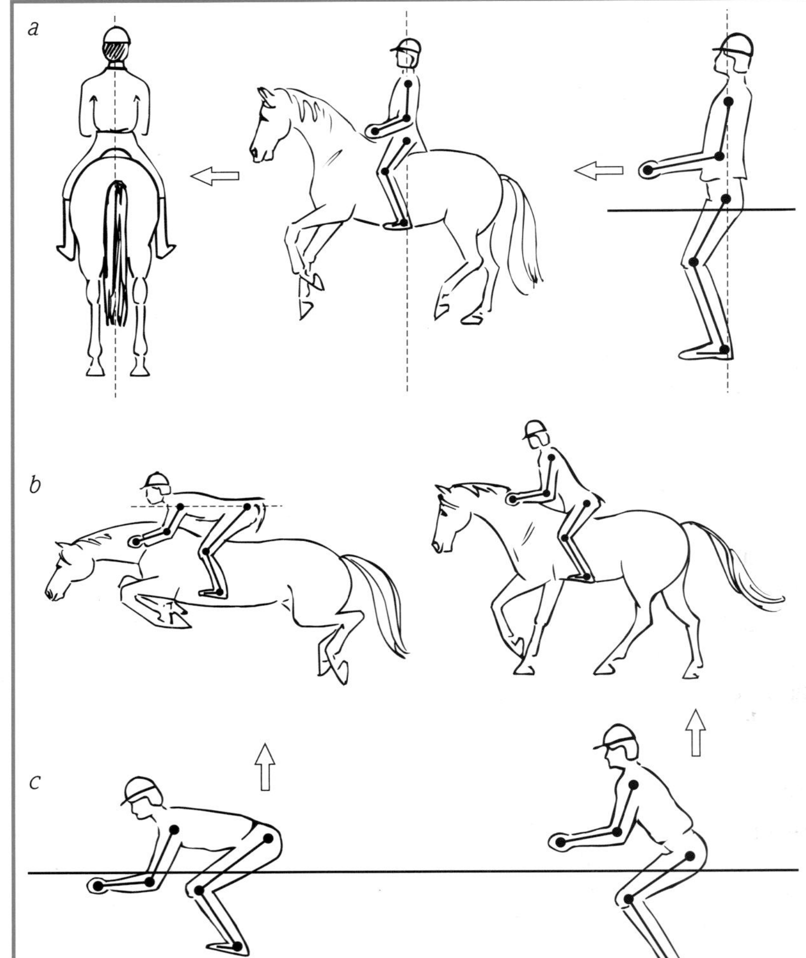

a. Correct central seat. Shoulders and hips in line with those of the horse. Shoulder, hip and heel on the vertical line, which is maintained as the hand advances.

b. Relationship of the joints over the fence and when in the jumping, half seat.

c. Upward movement of the hip at speed and reduced movement when in the restraining position.

deep in the saddle. Breathe out tension – breathe in trust. Breathe out nervousness – breathe in calmness. Every horse will stand quietly if the rider is inwardly at peace with himself.

It is just the same at walk.

One allows the movement of the horse to flow through one's own body. Everything that the rider has done and felt during the sitting exercises should now be put into practice – the feeling of balance through an upright, but not stiff, upper body. The more comfortable and unrestricted the rider sits, the more calmly his hands will hold the reins and be able to maintain a constant elastic band effect with the horse's mouth. Even when riding at the walk, it is still necessary to breathe in and out consciously and evenly.

Seat at Trot

The walk is the easiest pace in which to feel and maintain the correct seat as it is a pace without swing.

If we have learned to breathe and sit relaxed in the saddle with plenty of confidence, then the trot will give few problems so long as the movement of the horse is allowed to swing through the hip joints. We should now be ready to learn the rising trot. This kind of trot is a relief for both horse and rider. The first exercises should be carried out whilst standing so that the beginner is better prepared for the rising trot. Following the directions of the instructor, who will count 'one' then 'two', the rider lifts himself a little from the saddle and on 'two' lets himself down gently onto the saddle again. The rider should do this as much as possible with both hands on the hips, and when lifting up from the saddle should use both stirrups as supports; this is also a good exercise for balance.

The rider can also count to himself – later this can be done automatically in the mind – so as to lift himself and to descend evenly and so adapt to the trot rhythm with its diagonal step sequence. Supporting the hands on the hips will help to keep the balance. If the rider falls back into the saddle on rising and cannot remain standing in the stirrups, then the legs will slip forwards and he will no longer be balanced. He will then try to regain the balance by using the reins, a mistake which can easily become a habit that is difficult to rectify.

If the rider has such problems with balance at the very beginning, he can try resting both hands on the neck of the horse and resting the weight on the hands; standing up and sitting down will then be a little easier.

Once the student has mastered the rising and sitting exercises while the horse is standing and carries them out in a loosened position without tension, he must then try the same when the horse is at trot. The riding instructor asks the horse to trot and lets the rider stand up and sit down rhythmically, with the upper body bent slightly forward and the hands on hips. In doing this the pupil should be careful to trot on the correct diagonal, which will be the case if they sit down when the horse's inside hind leg is on the ground. In order to make certain of this, the rider will need to glance over the horse's outside shoulder: if it goes forward, then the rider has to lift himself out of the saddle, if it goes back, he has to sit down.

After this beginning the rider may perhaps feel somewhat stiff in the muscles of the upper leg and back. This quite natural occurrence will soon disappear, and even more quickly if the time between each riding lesson is short. If possible at the beginning, one should try to go on a three-week riding course at a reputable riding school where it is possible to take part in active riding every day. During this time, when one can get away from everyday life and concentrate just on riding, so much can be learned that one will perhaps already be able to control a horse and when at home can then sit on a different horse in a riding club and just join their riding lessons. After such an intensive course the beginners will soon be able to judge whether or not they want to continue with riding as a sport and recreation. Anyone not having the opportunity to take part in a course should try to take three riding lessons a week for four weeks in succession. After that they can spread out the intervals between lessons as they wish and according to time available.

After this short digression we return again to the riding lesson. Of course, the riding instructor will not let the pupil do rising trot for the whole lesson, but will include breaks at walk, depending on the fitness of the rider.

Seat at Canter

The next gait to be practised is the canter, a rocking-horse movement in a three-time beat. With a little support it should not be too difficult for the rider to learn how to canter by placing the inner hand on the pommel of the saddle whilst the outer hand holds the cantle. This will give the rider a firm grip. The riding instructor will bring the horse out of trot and into a canter after having explained to the pupil the new position of the legs for canter: inside leg lies near the girth and the outside one at least a hand's width behind the girth.

Again the front hand of the rider should continue to pull him back into the saddle so that the buttocks remain in the saddle and do not bounce up and down. With increasing confidence the rider will gradually release the hand from the rear of the saddle and later the other hand from the front of the saddle.

Again the riding instructor will insert breaks at walk into the lesson as too much cantering will be very tiring for the beginner. If his pupils can canter without the support of the hands after a few lessons, the instructor will then ask them to either put their hands on their hips, hold them out sideways or to let them hang down on the upper legs in order to establish the balance even more.

Aids and their Application

Until now the horse has been made to move to each pace or brought to a halt by a lunge whip or the voice of the instructor. Now the pupil must learn – while still on the lunge – to have direct effect on the horse for the first time, this is called applying the aids. The pupil will take on an active role in order to ask the horse to move forward from the halt. To do this the horse must be 'driven' or 'pushed' forward from the legs. The two legs are applied with an equal squeeze on the sides of the horse's body. If the horse does not respond to this, the squeeze is increased; if this still does not help the rider must increase it to a series of vibrato kicks with the legs. For a sensitive horse a slight squeeze is usually enough, but lazy horses require stronger leg aids. This applies not only to moving off, but to the whole spectrum of movement. If a horse does not move actively enough and trots along sluggishly, the rider then drives it with both legs. When cantering, the horse should be driven only with the inside leg on the girth, whilst the outer leg remains 1-2 hands width behind the girth on the body of the horse. The impulse to start the canter is brought about exclusively with the inside leg, whereas the outside leg has a holding effect. In riding language the inside leg is called the driving leg and the outside leg the controlling leg. In this way the young rider will learn to start to canter from the trot or from the walk. Every well-trained horse will accept these aids and begin to canter. When the rider has come so far then they can ask the horse to walk, trot and canter. They must also be able to stop the horse again, i.e. to bring it from a higher to a lower pace, which is called 'a downward transition'. To do this the contact with the horse's mouth is made a little stronger by taking the reins a little. This procedure of the hands has a restraining effect on the forward movement and is called a half-halt. The horse will respond to this and conform.

The instructor will insist continually that the pupil gets the widest part of the ball of the foot in the stirrup, the leg hangs loosely and the heel automatically takes the lowest point. In this way a deep seat is secured. Only when the rider sits 'in' the horse, rather than 'on' the animal, and drives from above to below, will the effect on the horse be complete.

The Aids in Concert

The use of the aids by the rider means the integrated employment of the leg, weight and rein aids. These are supported by the use of the voice and the whip. Through a moderate squeeze of the leg, the driving aid is produced. This can be on one or both sides of the horse. On the circle using one leg produces a driving aid. The other leg does not drive, but acts statically in a supporting position on the horse's body.

The following pictures show how leg, weight and rein aids work in the various lessons up to a preliminary level.

In the halt the rider puts even pressure on both seat bones. The legs lie evenly on the horse in order to prevent the horse from moving sideways or lining up crookedly. When the horse comes to a halt, the rider gives gently with the hand but without giving up the contact with the horse's mouth. To move off from the halt, for the transition from walk to trot, and to increase the tempo in walk and trot, the rider uses both sides of the driving leg aids and both seat-bones as weight aids. The effect of these driving aids must be accompanied by giving the reins a little, without giving up the contact with the horse's mouth. The elastic band effect must remain.

If the tempo at the walk or trot is not to change then the rider keeps an even and constant contact with the horse's mouth, braces the back slightly, and acts continuously with both legs. In the rising trot the rider lifts himself from deep knees and heels when the inside hind leg and the outside shoulder and foreleg swing forwards. The rider sits down during the support of the diagonal pair of legs on the inside hind foot. The rider only drives the horse when seated.

The weight aids can be light or heavy. Sitting in the normal posture the weight aid is heavy. If both seat bones are of equal weight, then the weight aids will be on both sides. When one seat bone is applied more than the other, it is called a one-sided weight aid. With the one-sided weight aid it is easy for the rider to make the mistake of bending at the hips. In doing this, the rider gains a mistaken impression of having the weight on one side, whereas in reality the opposite is happening, i.e. the weight of the rider is, in fact, going in the other direction.

Taking, giving, retaining, controlling are all ways in which the rein aids are used. In taking the rein aid the little fingers are guided a little towards the body, and in giving them a little away from the body. If after taking the rein aids there is to be no giving of the rein and the aid is sustained, this is called retaining. When the horse is positioned or bent, the inside rein is taken a little and the outside one given a little to allow the outside shoulder to go forward and also to control the amount of bend in the head and the neck.

When beginning to canter the rider first positions the horse slightly inwards. The inside driving leg is placed on the girth and the outside controlling leg a little behind the girth. The

Applying the Aids – Halt

In the halt the rider puts his weight equally on both seat bones. Both legs lie equally on the horse, in order to prevent stepping sideways or a crooked line-up.

If the horse has come to a halt, the rider gives a little with the hand, but keeps contact with the horse's mouth.

Riding off from Halt

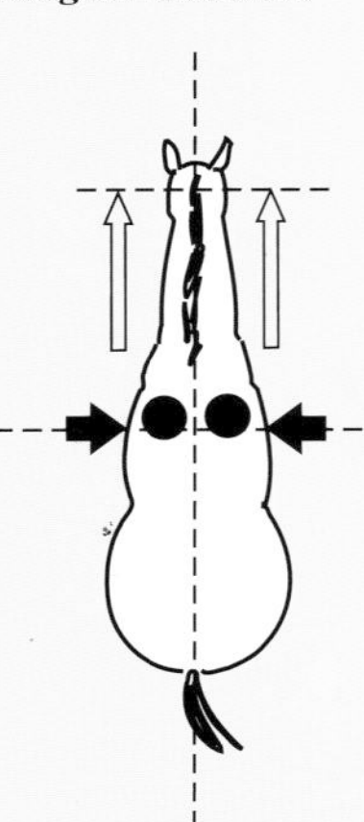

The hand gives for a moment in order to bring the driving aids into effect.

Walk and trot without increasing the tempo (tempo = the speed of the rhythm).

Rein back (a ridden horse) 1st Phase

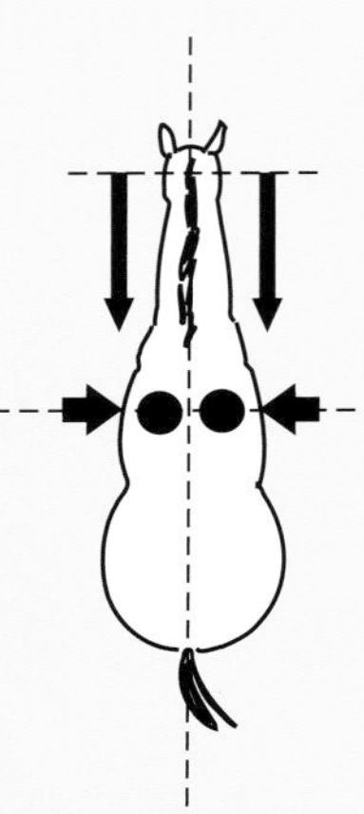

The hand keeps a constant contact with the horse's mouth. The back is slightly braced, the effect of the leg is continuously maintained.

Beginning to Canter (left)

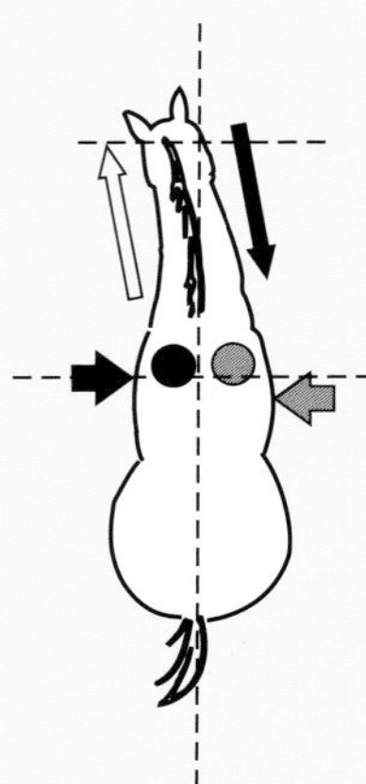

At the moment of beginning to canter the inside (left) hand gives for a short moment in order to release the stride into canter.

Canter without changing tempo (left canter)

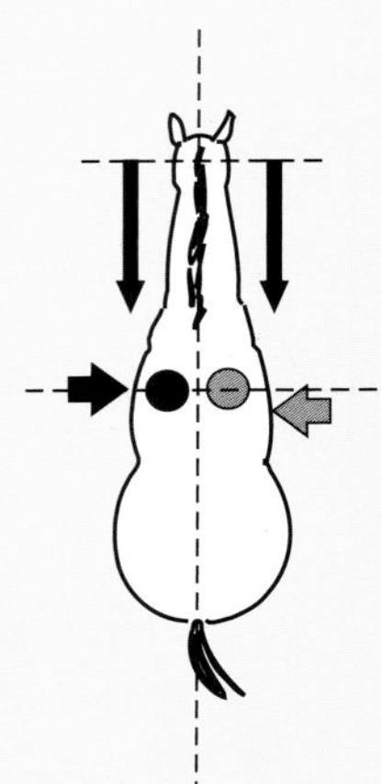

The inside (left) seat bone applies more weight. The inside driving leg keeps or stimulates the liveliness of the canter stride.

Halts – Transitions 1st Phase

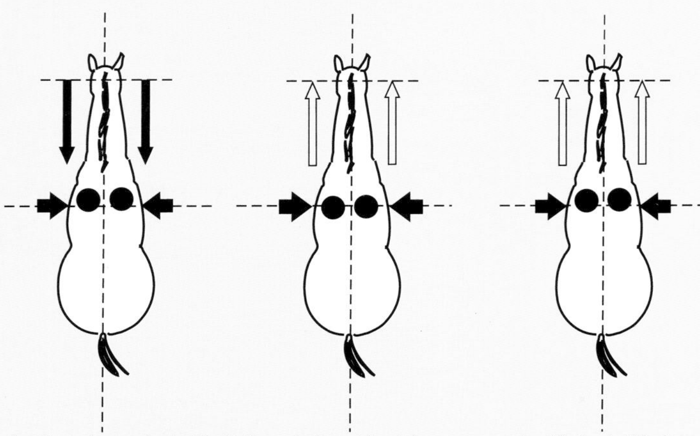

In the first phase of a half-halt the rein is retained for a moment until the half-halt is complete. After this in the second phase the hand gives immediately without, however, giving up the contact to the horse's mouth. The whole halt consists of a series of half-halts following each other. To increase the tempo at walk and trot the hand gives in order to release the effect of the driving aids to maximum effect.

Rising Trot – Sitting

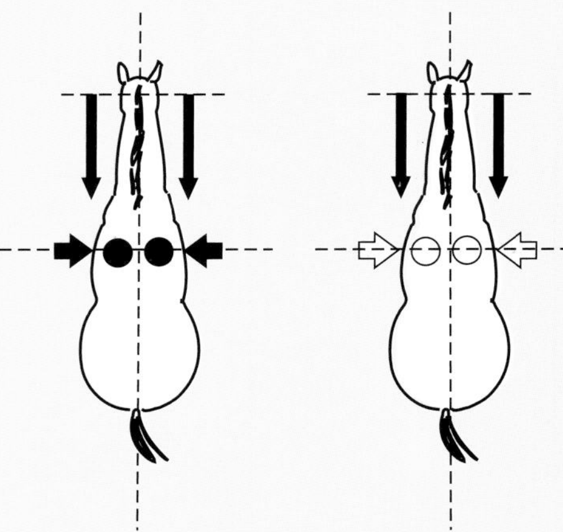

When the rider lifts his seat from the saddle, the leg, with a deep knee and heel, remains on the horse's body, but has, at this moment, no driving effect. The rising trot is practised equally on both diagonals.

When the legs are applied the hand gives in order to release the effect of the driving aids.

Sitting trot allows for an increase in the rider's influence. The seat remains in the saddle with the hips leading the movement and a supple, undulating back absorbing it.

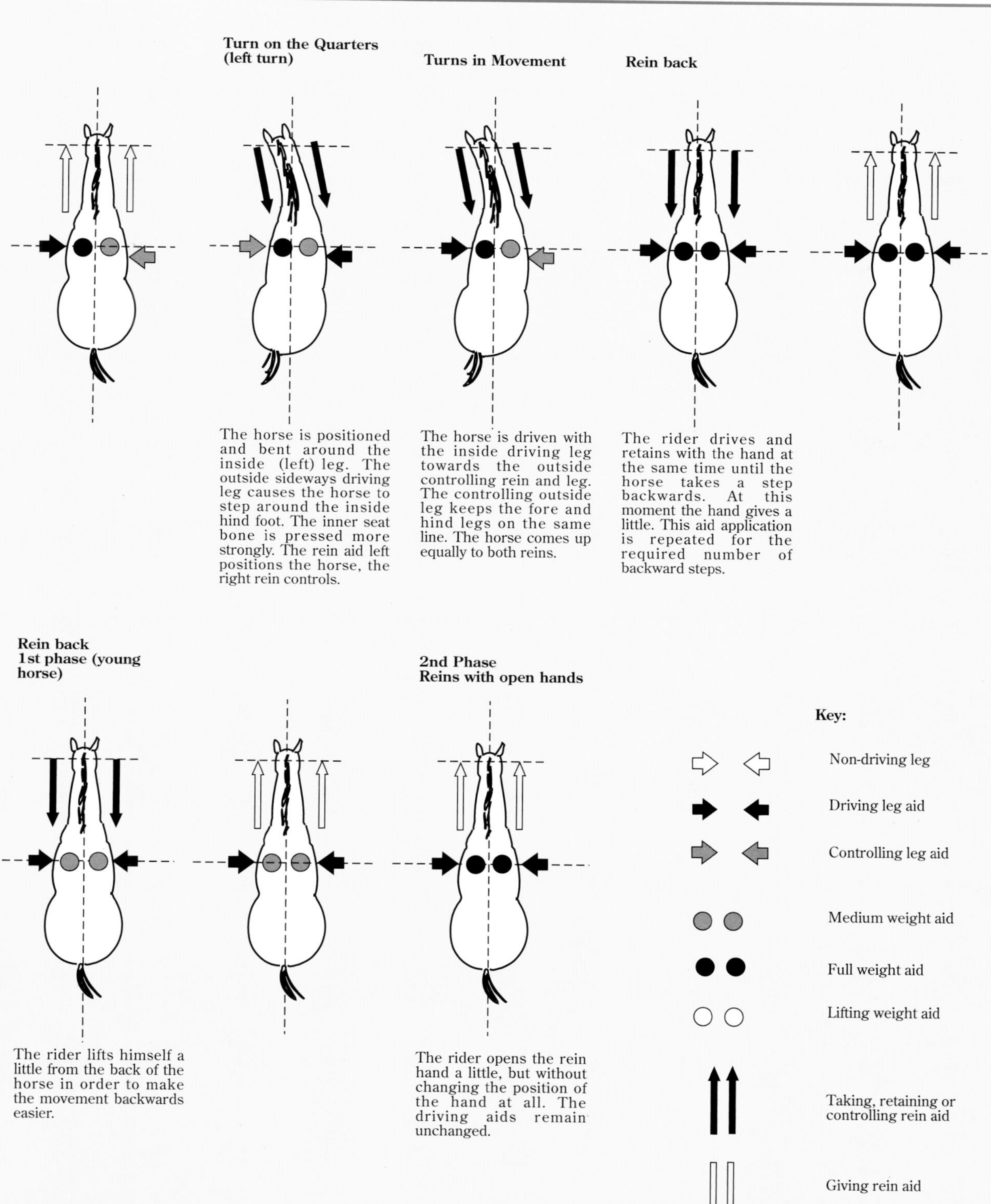
Turn on the Quarters (left turn)
Turns in Movement
Rein back
The horse is positioned and bent around the inside (left) leg. The outside sideways driving leg causes the horse to step around the inside hind foot. The inner seat bone is pressed more strongly. The rein aid left positions the horse, the right rein controls.
The horse is driven with the inside driving leg towards the outside controlling rein and leg. The controlling outside leg keeps the fore and hind legs on the same line. The horse comes up equally to both reins.
The rider drives and retains with the hand at the same time until the horse takes a step backwards. At this moment the hand gives a little. This aid application is repeated for the required number of backward steps.
Rein back 1st phase (young horse)
2nd Phase Reins with open hands
The rider lifts himself a little from the back of the horse in order to make the movement backwards easier.
The rider opens the rein hand a little, but without changing the position of the hand at all. The driving aids remain unchanged.
Key:
Non-driving leg
Driving leg aid
Controlling leg aid
Medium weight aid
Full weight aid
Lifting weight aid
Taking, retaining or controlling rein aid
Giving rein aid

inside seat bone is applied more and when beginning the canter, upon squeezing from the inside leg, the inside hand gives for a moment in order to release the canter stride. When cantering the horse is positioned straight and the rider sits consciously on the inside seat bone. When increasing the tempo of the canter the hand gives to allow the driving aids to take proper effect. Half-halts are introduced in order to change from a higher to a lower pace, to reduce tempo, to bring the horse by an even tempo to a lighter submission to the rider's hand, to make the horse attentive to a lesson, and to improve the outline and carriage of the horse. The full halt consists of a series of half-halts, following one after the other, that will bring the horse from moving to a halt. In halt both legs drive together and the rider braces the back more. At the same time the rider takes the reins a little and keeps them for a short time until the completion of the halt. Then the hand gives again without losing the contact with the horse's mouth, and the back and leg aids are reduced.

In the turn on the quarters the horse is positioned around the inside leg and bent in the direction of the movement. The outside, sidewards driving leg turns the horse around the inside hind foot. The inside seat bone applies more pressure. The inside rein aid positions the horse and the outside rein controls. When the horse is well-ridden there will be a light submission.

When making a turn while the horse moves forward, the horse is driven with the inside driving leg into the outside controlling rein and leg. Depending on the curvature of the turn the horse will be bent around the inside leg. However, the inside leg should not drive sideways, but is used to cause the hind foot to step further forwards. The controlling leg will make sure that the front and hind legs will remain on the same line. The inside seat bone applies more pressure and the inside rein is taken a little. The outside rein is adjusted to let the outside shoulder go forward and then arrests the effect of the inside driving aids by controlling them.

For the rein back the rider applies the same driving weight and leg aids equally on both sides, as when starting to move forwards. The reins will have not a giving but a retaining effect until the horse takes the first step backwards. The reins are then immediately given a little in order to repeat the giving and taking until the required number of steps have been achieved. With a young horse the rider can assist the stepping backwards by lightly taking the weight off the back.

To obtain free walk on a long rein, the rider opens the hand without changing the driving weight and leg aids. The hand then maintains a light contact with the horse's mouth. The well-ridden horse will then stretch the neck forwards and down, which should be done slowly without the horse snatching itself free from the rein.

Application and Effect of the Leg Aids

Driving forwards

From the back to the front – in the transition from halt to moving, for increasing tempo – activating the hindquarter activity (impulse-collection) – at times more effective in a position close to the girth (rule of thumb: the front edge of the boot should be almost at the back edge of the girth) both sides.
e.g. at medium trot – extended trot.

Driving sidewards

Retains the turn – securing the order of movements sidewards – forwards. Leg shifts – rectangle reducing – enlarging. Forehand turn – turn on haunches.

Controlling

Guarantees the walking of the horse in a straight line in all turns – canter – counter canter.

Application and Effect of Weight Aids

Weight on both sides

Exclusively forwards driving (e.g. start riding – increasing tempo) – half-halt – maintain the swing – activating the hindquarters (collection).

Weight one side

Canter – turns.

Lightening the weight

Lifting off (rising trot).

Application and Effect of the Rein Aids

Rein aids

1. **Giving:** Increasing the length of the outline. Medium and fast tempo, e.g. medium trot, extended trot. Exchange of taking and giving in full and half-halts.

2. **Taking:**
See half-halts.

3. **Retaining:** Regular and constant contact between rider's hand and horse's mouth. Improvement of the receptiveness through increased driving towards the maintaining hand.

4. **Controlling:** Limiting the turn, keeping the position and bending, half-halts, regulating the time, transition to a higher or lower tempo, tempo difference, improving outline and carriage of the horse, introduction and preparation for new lessons/movements, rein back.

Full Halt

Halting from any pace.

Group Riding

When the beginner on the lunge has become confident enough, and has learned actively to have an effect on the horse, then the riding instructor will take him into the first stages of riding in the arena. Riding behind an experienced beginner will be the simplest way for a rider to try out what has been learned and to put it into practice in some measure on his own. In the arena the school horses will follow the instinct of the herd and the voice of the riding instructor and move calmly and regularly one after another. The rider therefore will have the possibility to occasionally be passive and concentrate on the seat. When riding in a group the beginner will learn to lead and regulate the horse so that they remain a safe distance from the person in front and can execute the various school figures correctly.

Riding Alone

When the rider has gained confidence in riding in a group the riding instructor will let him carry out exercises on his own. Now a precise application of aids is necessary and so the independence of the rider is tested and encouraged. Confident riding alone is the pre-requisite for the first riding in open country.

Learning in a group in an arena allows the rider to gain confidence and concentrate on his riding posture.

Structure of the Lesson

A riding lesson will generally be divided into three parts of 20 minutes each:

1. Warming-up and preparation phase.
2. Working phase.
3. Finishing and relaxation phase.

1. Loosening-up and warming-up exercises for rider and horse: walk on a long rein, rising trot, riding large turns, tempo differences.
   Do not forget to readjust the girth!
2. Learning new lessons and exercises to improve and refine the use of aids.

A short break should take place just before the end of the working phase, finishing with a final exercise that the horse and rider will have completed well because each lesson should be concluded with something successful for both horse and rider.

3. Ride on a loose rein, praise the horse, ride at walk, ride or lead the horse in the open country as much as possible.

The Riding School

The riding school is an open or covered rectangle of 20 x 40 or 20 x 60 metres with two long and two short sides.

The outside boundary is call the rail. Along the rails runs the track, which can generally be recognised as a trodden-down furrow. About 1.5 metres alongside it lies the second, or inner, track.

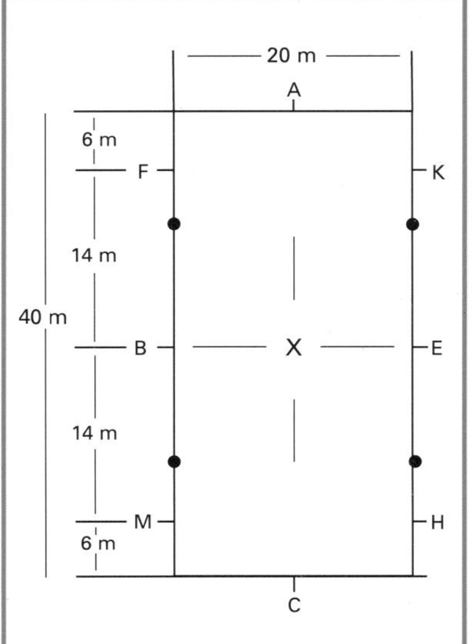

Important Notes:

Inside is the side of the track that faces inward; outside is the ride facing the rail; if one rides on the right hand, then one rides round to the right (clockwise); if one rides on the left hand, then one rides round to the left (anti-clockwise); the school is divided up and marked at different points with letters that provide marking points for school figures.

Rules in the School

In the school certain rules apply that are essential for the safety of both rider and horse:

When entering the arena or leaving it, one calls 'door open' and waits for a response.

Mounting and dismounting is done in the centre of the school.

At the walk the track is always kept free except when a group is being ridden.

Without exception 'priority' is always given to riders on the left hand.

If there are a lot of riders in the arena, it is better that they all ride on the same rein.

Then the riding instructor or senior rider will, after 5 minutes, call for a change of rein.

In the arena the same safety and courtesy rules apply as for instance in skiing: consideration, care, forbearance.

Always be considerate towards young horses and inexperienced riders: the experienced rider is much more able to control the horse than a beginner.

Always keep a sufficient distance behind the person in front.

Always keep sufficient distance at the side.

One distinguishes the following school figures:

Complete Track: CMBFAKEH
(right hand)

Half Track: CMBXEH
(right hand)

Long side: MF or KH
(right hand)

Short Side: both sides C or both sides A.

Centre line (length or track): CXA or AXC.

Changing line, through the whole track: MXK or FXH.

Changing line through the half track: ME or FE or KB or HB.

Middle Point of the Arena: X.

Circle: It is a circle of 20 metres diameter. Riding a right-hand circle starting at C, the points of the circle that the rider must touch for a length of a horse are the middle between the corner after C and B (10m), at X and the middle between E and the corner before H (10m). The second circle is the same between A and X.

To change out of the circle: after completing a circle the rider rides through the point X and then directly onto the second circle.

Changing through the circle: the rider turns away on the circle point on the long side in a circle bend of 10m diameter, rides through the middle point of the circle and returns in a circle bend of 10m diameter to the circle line.

Changing points are the points M, F, K and H.

Simple serpentine: an evenly bent line along the long side, that distances itself a maximum of 6 steps (approx 5m) from the long side. It begins at the first changing point and ends at the following changing point on the long side.

Double serpentine: this is carried out on the long side and distances itself twice for up to a maximum of 3 steps from the long side. It begins on the first changing point on the long side, touches the track at B or E with a horse length, and ends at the following changing point. Both ends must be equal. Loop serpentines through the whole arena: here the number of loops can differ according to the test. When riding, for example, five loops the rider must touch the track on the long sides besides the changing point three times, each time with a horse's length.

Volte is a circle of 6 steps (approx 5m) diameter.

Coming out of the corner: this is a turn that is ridden like a half a Volte of 6 steps (approx 5m) and after approximately 9 steps ends towards the long side.

Double Volte: a volte carried out twice, one after another.

Figure of eight: a volte on the right (left) hand followed directly by a volte on the left (right) hand. It is always carried out in the centre of the arena at X.

A basic knowledge about the behaviour of horses is just as important as knowledge about anatomy and physiology. All theoretical knowledge lacks the relationship to the horse and the pleasure and ease that we can only experience in actual association.

It is not just the riding that should bring with it happiness and relaxation, but the whole process of being occupied with the wonderful being of the horse that should bring us back to nature and occupy ourselves with things that we have not consciously noticed before. All this will only be possible when riding is no longer a drain on our energies making us tired and exhausted, but gives us a feeling of oneness with the horse and with nature so that we get caught up in the flow of movements, in the agility of a cantering horse. Then riding becomes an unforgettable experience.

Countryside school means:
Rider and horse in unified trust getting used to natural surroundings.

Training in the countryside is essential for both horse and rider, and must not be confused with early trips taken with beginners.

Riding in open countryside even if it means organising a riding holiday in a suitable area is part of the learning curve for both horse and rider.

It is probable that school riding has become an end in itself, which is a pity, because it should be a means to an end, the school disciplines preparing the horse and rider for riding in the countryside and enjoying the natural environment.

However, there has to be a discipline in recreational riding of this sort. Riders must, for instance, keep to recognised bridlepaths and must observe the code of the countryside.

Where facilities exist for riders to go on farm-type rides providing a variety of optional obstacles they should be used and welcomed as opportunities for both horse and rider to relax and enjoy themselves. Almost all horses will be encouraged by being a member of a group and in these circumstances will tackle moderate-sized obstacles and natural hazards with enthusiasm.

Working on the lunge to the left. The whip is changed over to the right hand.

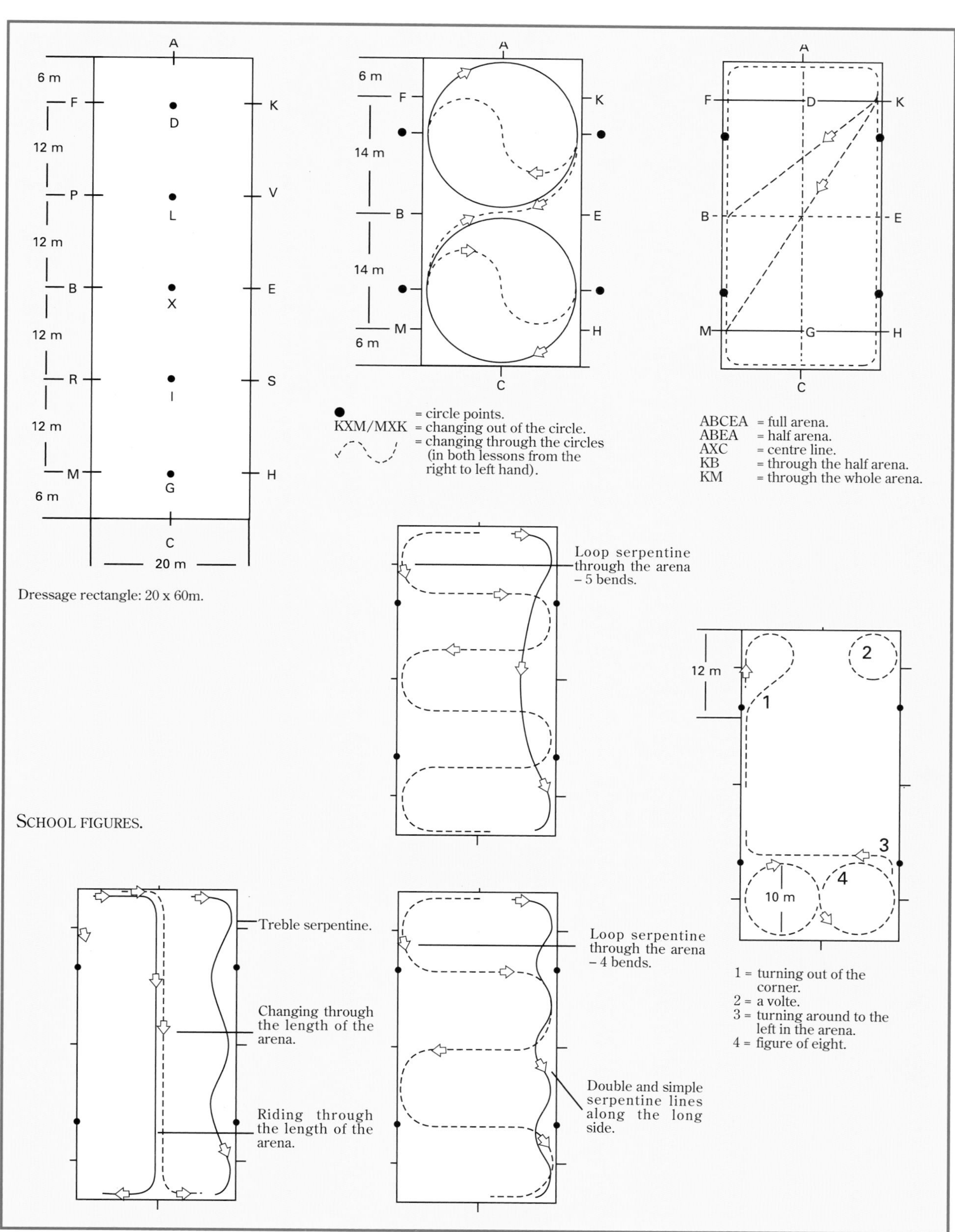

SCHOOL FIGURES.

The Half-seat

The light seat or half-seat used for cross-country riding and jumping eases both horse and rider. The stirrups are shortened 2-4 holes to give a sharper angle in the knee joints and the hips. Whilst mounted with the horse standing, the rider tries the shorter stirrups with closed knees and the upper body leaning slightly forward to bring the body into a balance. The hands rest left and right around the neck of the horse. The elbows are at an angle.

The rider now tries to stay in this position and imagine a gentle wave motion that is pushed from the knees and the buttocks. The rider should imagine the motion of the canter and practice this on the horse or as a gymnastic training on the ground.

By placing the weight into the right or left knee, the rider is in a position to make changes of direction by using the weight aids. A good light seat encourages both rider and horse equally. Bouncing buttocks and an unbalanced rider make the canter through the countryside a much less enjoyable experience for the horse.

To attain a light seat more easily and to prepare for learning how to ride cross-country, a grid is used. This consists of poles on the ground spaced about 5-6ft apart. At the trot the rider in the shorter, jumping seat trots energetically, relaxed and evenly over the poles. If the horse begins to canter, let it do so. His position will be absolutely calm and the rider adjusts flexibly into the movement of the horse. The buttocks remain slightly above the saddle, the weight of the rider rests in the deep knees and in the stirrups. The rider can remain calm because he has understood that the whole movement of the horse is absorbed by springy, loose knee and hip joints. The hands should remain calmly at the neck with a finger of each hand holding the neckstrap. With this aid the rider learns, using the elbow, to go in the direction of the horse's mouth, without moving the hands from their position. Anyone making their first attempts over small obstacles in this way will sooner or later obtain optimum harmony with the horse to jump over fixed obstacles in jumping or in country riding. The calmer the rider can remain in this position and also maintain a good balance on the horse, the less the horse will be disturbed in its natural technique of negotiating obstacles. The voice of the rider is far more important than the driving leg application or correction with the reins. Any aid applied before or after an obstacle disturbs the concentration of the horse.

It is helpful to have a lead horse in front of the beginner in order to get the right feel for the correct tempo. Every horse has in itself its own ideal tempo. This has something to do with the volume that the horse has to move. Without a certain basic

Cross-country riding means that the rider and horse must work in perfect harmony. Training is important and this form of riding should not be undertaken until some experience has been acquired.

tempo in the canter a horse will not be able to clear obstacles, and cannot lengthen the canter stride necessary for jumping. A horse should not get faster before taking a jump, but the canter stride should be lengthened with more propulsion from the hocks. Every jump is just a lengthened canter stride.

If we keep these ideas in our head and let this picture work on us in the canter, we come into the right canter rhythm of the horse almost instinctively. We feel then, if we listen carefully within ourselves, when the horse begins to feel good. Many riders never achieve this feeling because they are afraid of speed. Every horse has an inner clock, that creates its own canter rhythm. We know that horses run away or bolt simply as a result of fear or panic, which can be triggered off by the rider's bad behaviour. It should be clear to us all, that a horse only bolts when we do something wrong. Once the rider has mastered the pole grid a small cross-pole fence can be erected 10-12ft from the last element of the grid.

Another aid in the light seat that should be practised from the very beginning is for the rider to place his weight into the left knee and look left, the horse will follow him. When the rider brings the weight into the right knee and looks right, the horse will follow. More about this in the chapter on jump training.

The elastic band principle in the contact to the horse's mouth can be felt even better because going along with it comes directly from the elbows. Should a horse rush away, then the rider should brace himself in the saddle and stop it with a calm voice and deep hand. When riding in a group always come to a halt when a rider has problems. Horses are herd animals and they remain together.

Anyone who goes out with their horse for any length of time and has treated their horse properly will learn all the different kinds of behaviour and also notice very quickly that jumping over small obstacles is the most natural thing in the world for horses to do. The only thing we should not do is let something like a tree stump cause us to become frightened, because that

fear will be transmitted to the horse. Small children on their ponies, for example, can follow any of the larger horses because they are not afraid and take everything in their stride. However, the rider's body should remain balanced and adjust harmoniously to the horse's balance.

Horses are also our instructors when jumping. We only need to support them in all their natural instinctive behaviour and not divert them from their natural harmonious balance.

Riding Up and Down Hill

New demands are made upon both horse and rider in hilly countryside. Nevertheless, undulating countryside especially makes riding a great experience. Horses like to take small hills with a swing and can be allowed to canter away. The rider remains in the half-seat in order to take the weight from the horse's back as much as possible. The hand should give sufficient freedom to let the neck become longer, without, however, giving up contact to the horse's mouth altogether. The horse needs this long neck in order to balance itself and steep slopes nearly always need to be taken at walk or canter. At a canter, when the horse needs plenty of swing in order to get up the hill, the hands should hold on to the neck strap. For long climbs the rider should adopt whatever pace the horse offers him. If the riding instructor is present he will know exactly the capabilities of the horse and its condition, so that the rider can rely on these instructions. It is particularly tiring to the horse when riders put undue weight onto the horse's back with their seat when they should be trying to close the knees and put the weight in the stirrups.

The gentle pleasure of the walk.

It is important to note that a steep slope incline should always be ridden straight up, and the same applies to a downhill slope.

Riding steep downhill slopes should be done at walk as the strain is particularly great on the front legs. Here the contact to the horse's mouth must always be kept stronger in order to give the horse support, particularly when the descent is very steep. To avoid a slip sideways the horse must be kept absolutely straight throughout the descent. At the beginning, young riders are reluctant when riding downhill to place the upper body forwards in order to take the weight off the horse's back. But this position is absolutely essential because this is the only way that the horse can balance himself properly and get the hindquarters under the body.

Jumping

The young rider can start to jump when he has learned the beginnings of the half-seat and is in a position to give effective commands to the horse. When jumping over low or high obstacles it is essential that there is harmony between rider and horse, and balance is decisive in this. When horses jump without a rider, they regulate their own tempo and the pace according to the height of the jump and their experience and disposition. If the rider upsets the self-confidence and the skill of a horse, both horse and rider become unsure. Even experienced jumpers and instructors will have all had to learn how to jump and know that at the beginning there are some inhibitions to be overcome.

Driving Aids

For the next exercise in jumping, two poles are erected at a distance from 7m to 7.5m and at a height of 30cm. A horse used to this will not see a height of 30cm as a jump at all and may well trot over it; another pole can be placed across the top of the

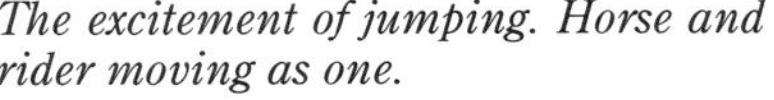

The excitement of jumping. Horse and rider moving as one.

grid. These small jumps have wings to prevent the horse from trying to run out sideways. The rider should concentrate exclusively on these two jumps. It is recommended that an experienced rider should first demonstrate how to ride these fences so that the beginner can see how it should be accomplished. All the riders line up on the track and the instructor explains the procedure. The jumps of individual riders can then be discussed: learn through consciously watching.

The exercise is done in the jumping seat at trot. If a horse does not go forward freely into the fence the rider will need to resort to his driving aids. The upper body must remain in front of the vertical and the rider needs to drive the horse more with an active leg.

If a horse get a little impetuous before the jump then the rider must remain passive in the jumping seat, check quietly with the rein and concentrate on making a straight approach.

Approach

As a result of making only small demands at the beginning, the rider will have learned gradually to achieve a harmonious calmness in the balance when jumping. The support in the stirrup and the firm closed knee gives the rider confidence and thus they become increasingly effective in the use of the aids. The jump will improve if the rider drives before the obstacle. A horse should be brought calmly to the obstacle and by increased driving before the jump the canter stride will be lengthened and the jump made with increased freedom.

It is not the height of the jumps that is important in training but the precise execution of them. Anyone able to accomplish low jumps well and with confidence will later be able to manage the greater demands of height. For this reason it is particularly important that a rider takes his horse smoothly between the various obstacles and can ride the required tracks. The rider should negotiate the turns correctly and ensure that the horse does not evade by wavering too far inwards or outwards. If a horse moves inwards then the inner leg must work against it supported by the rein aids; the inner hand remains at the neck, without going over the withers on the outside, and the outer hand leads the horse a little outwards.

If the horse pulls itself outwards, then the opposite aids must be used. Only a good direction of line will make a straight approach to the jump possible.

If the instructor makes an obstacle inviting, then jumping it will be much easier for horse and rider. A distance pole placed before the fence makes it easier for both horse and rider to measure the stride. The rider must train himself to have an eye

Perfect partnerships – Above: *Wonderful technique in all three photographs demonstrating perfect posture and leg positioning.*
Below far left: *Excellent hand position but the rider's legs are a little too far back.*
Left: *Perfect symmetry.*

for the approach, as correcting efforts just before the jump have a disturbing effect on the horse. In the early jumping lessons the experienced horse will take over the measuring.

In this exercise the horse will regulate the tempo itself. After jumping over the first grid it will take two canter strides and will find nearly the same take-off point in front of the next grid pyramid.

Use of the Whip

A whip for jumping should not be longer that 80cm. The use of the whip when jumping is something one must learn. When making the first few jumps the young rider will be very much

A perfect jump.

taken up with himself so that he will not be able to make sensible use of it. In the arena the rider will always hold the whip on the inside in order to support the inside leg. The wall will be the outer line of demarcation for the obstacles. The whip serves as a support to the driving aids and should be held with the hand slightly inwards. The hand should in no way disturb the horse's mouth and so restrict the forward movement whilst using the whip as a tap on the shoulder. Even the motorist does not put his foot on the accelerator and brake at the same time.

Jumping demands determination and some courage. With a good seat, confidence, and proper instruction anyone can learn to jump. The controlled, decisive riding towards a jump will carry over to the horse, who by nature has the disposition to jump and enjoys it at the same time, provided it has learned to jump under proper instruction. The horse is courageous and reliable if not disturbed by the rider. A rider with a particular talent for jumping will, if the horse has the right aptitude, be able to attempt higher fences, negotiate more difficult courses and participate in competitions.

Harmony when Jumping

The right tempo when cantering, the feeling for the canter rhythm and the lightness of the springy jumping seat, the 'elastic band principle', the submission to the horse's mouth that gives optimum balance to everything, are the important building bricks to harmony when jumping. If all these components are finely tuned with each other and the ingredients are correctly selected, then harmony between the two will follow. When jumping it is not the height of the jump that is decisive nor the placement. It is more important that jumping is a pleasure for both horse and rider and if the basics are understood and the individual components are put together, this is far more important than technical-tactical riding in which every centimetre of the horse's stride is precisely controlled by the rider. The co-operation of powers that are triggered through the imagination and our thoughts can reveal themselves now in the entire course of movements of the horse. It will canter in an energetic rhythm, approach the jumps appropriately, and clear them with ease, land and canter away without breaking the flow of the movement. We must learn to think in pictures with the horse. This means consciously seeing good examples, receiving them into ourselves and visualising them in our mind. One day our movements will be in tune with our feelings and thoughts and in harmony will melt together with the horse. If we used the power of our mind more, we could all achieve top performances.

There are different styles of jumping – but the rider must always ride to the harmony of the horse.

Dressage

Dressage does not mean training a horse in the same way one would train a dog, it means to put the horse through gymnastic exercises. Every part of the body, each member and muscle must be exercised, built up and strengthened in an appropriate sequence. Sensible work with the horse and its increasing responsiveness will also make it become obedient.

Responsiveness means that the driving as well as the halting aids (the downward transitions) with their desired effects are accepted by the horse.

Proficiency grades are set by a series of tests approved by the national organising body. Clearly, they vary a little between one country and the other but essentially the tests range between preliminary, introductory competitions, though medium levels to advanced.

International competitions including the Olympic competitions are governed by the FEI (Fédèration Èquestre Internationale) to which all the nations concerned with competitive equestrian sport belong. Those competitions are outside the scope of this book. We shall look at the sport in general terms as between the beginner and the more experienced rider.

The rider needs to school his body consciousness by the practice of remedial exercise that is combined with mental imagery. A simple form of yoga as it were.

Such exercises make it possible to recognise and change incorrect posture that has become a habit. If a rider has not noticed that for years they have walked and stood crookedly and bent, then being told that they sit crookedly on the horse will make the learning process much more difficult.

The rider must be made aware that marvellous changes and improvements can be accomplished in themselves and the horse if they become movement conscious. I want, nonetheless, to warn that such miracles do not happen overnight, they take a little longer than that. The consistent posture and behaviour pattern of the rider make it possible to execute the required gymnastic exercises on the horse. The rider must have a clear picture of how to sit on the horse, i.e. balanced, upright but independent, and should understand that regular breathing leads to mental calm. Deep, regular breathing will transfer peace and composure to the horse. We must consciously handle the horse and try to slow down our own sequence of movements.

The systematic correction of the picture in the mind of the rider is of more value than the correction of individual details that are pointed out by the teacher during the lesson.

Consciously or unconsciously riders all over the world and in all kinds of riding have used the meditative method to reach their goals. Mental training, indeed, is increasingly integral to many types of sport today.

The Training Scale

The natural movements of a horse must be maintained when carrying the weight of the rider. The horse should become relaxed in a balanced response to the rider's aids. In putting together a riding lesson there are six points to consider.
Looseness and Relaxation.
Rhythm.
Submission.
Swing.
Straightening.
Collection.

Looseness

Before the start of a competition every athlete will use warm-up and loosening exercises as a way of preparation. This loosening and

warming up must also be given to our horses. After mounting, the rider will walk on a loose rein. Next the rider takes up the reins and goes into rising trot until he feels that the tension in the horse has subsided. Working with grids greatly assists loosening up and also establishes the rhythm. Changing between trot and canter will often loosen the back muscles. Once the movement begins to swing the rider should feel sitting becomes more comfortable. As he works the horse will relax its neck muscles and seek contact with the rider's hand in a forwards and down stretch. As a check for total looseness it is a good idea to practise the open hand rein that advances in an arc over the horse's neck. As the hand advances with the horse the rider goes forward and the horse stretches forwards and down without losing the rhythm. Calm, regular movements with an active back and a tail carried without tension are indications of looseness. With a good stretching of the neck forwards and down the horse should move at walk, trot and canter without hurrying.

Rhythm

Rhythm is the regularity of movements in the three basic paces of walk, trot and canter. The walk is a pace without swing, a four-time

A rider at medium trot.

rhythm with eight phases of movement. Here the rhythm can be lost as a result of applying the rein too strongly so that the horse stiffens in the back, or it is ridden forwards too strongly and causes the stride to be extended beyond the natural physique or training. The result can be a walk that inclines to pacing, that is, the legs being moved in lateral rather than diagonal pairs.

The trot is a two-time rhythm in four phases. Here also a horse can lose the rhythm if the trot is pushed too far. If the trot is allowed to speed up and become out of balance, the rhythm is lost and the pace becomes hurried.

The canter is a three-time rhythm in six phases. If a rider attempts to over-check the canter stride through the hand, then the hind quarters will become insufficiently engaged. In this case, during the diagonal phase of the canter, the horse will often place one foot after the other – first hind, then fore – and canter in four-time. By letting the neck go forwards and maintaining the driving aids, the horse will easily return to a three-time pace.

The walk and the trot.

Submission

Submission is the result of even, constant contact of the rider's hand to the horse's mouth. When the rider takes up the reins a contact is made between the hands and the horse's mouth. Only as a result of a constant moving towards this contact will the horse stay on the bit, that is give way at the neck. The driving aids must be considerably stronger than the halting aids. The extent of the submission therefore has a close relationship to the driving application, which should always be light. In the case of stronger application and submission the rider must offer the horse a soft and feeling hand with continuous giving (elastic band feeling), that will cause the horse to yield.

Swing

In maintaining the rhythm a horse should move forwards with swing. If the rider increases the driving with the back and legs, without hurrying, the hindquarters are forced to stride energetically. The horse should not move dragging the hind legs, but engage them energetically under the body.

Due to the forward push of a swinging back, the rider is more easily positioned with the movement and obtains a deeper, more flexible seat. Changing tempo at the trot and at the canter help to improve the swing of the horse substantially. The swing is regulated by the appropriate half-halts. Here the harmony of the synchronisation of the aids is also important.

Straightening

The natural crookedness of the horse demands straightening. It is said that this crookedness is related to the position of the embryo in the mother's womb. This shows itself particularly on the right hand in canter. The hind legs do not track up to the imprint of the forelegs, rather the hind leg steps between the front legs and the right hind leg steps correspondingly inwards.

By plenty of riding on curved lines the horse can be brought onto both reins, it submits, and adjusts to the required turn. If the rider feels that the horse can execute the volte equally well on the left or the right, then it is straightened. If one rides on freshly raked soil, then the tracks of the fore and hind legs will be seen in one line, even in the volte.

Collection

More will be said about collection in a later chapter as it goes far beyond the standard of the novice horse and rider.

The individual points of the training are the prerequisites for the correct execution of a dressage test. The rider must be able to master them practically and theoretically and arrange his exercise periods accordingly. In a dressage test the horse must move unrestricted, swinging underneath the rider, constant on the reins, certain of the aids and obedient. The individual lessons described up to now are generally practised in schooling and training classes. A period of training, also called a training unit, is made up of:

Preparation – loosening up.
Main part – working.
Finish – relaxation.

The preparation – the loosening up, the period of which depends on the disposition of the horse itself – produces: the loosening up and relaxation of the muscles; suppleness, the gradual increase of heart and blood circulation; improvement in rhythm and impulsion and a calming effect on the horse.

In the main part of the training session, through appropriate lessons, the horse is increasingly put to the aids and its obedience is put to the test. With specific individual tasks the rider tries with fine tuned and correct execution to improve the exercise section. During the training session the rider is the actual trainer of the horse, as he must respond immediately to the horse's behaviour and way of going. The instructor can therefore only affect the development of the horse to a limited degree. The end of the training session should relax the rider and especially the horse and by a gradual transition from the intensity of the work, should return to a normal relaxed and

Working trot.

Medium trot.

Extended trot.

unrestrained movement (walk on a long rein). Psychological problems can best be worked out by a ride in the country.

If the development of the performance of horse and rider is to be tested, then attempting the lower grade dressage test is appropriate. Throughout the whole task the horse must be certain of the aids so that it is possible to go through the tempo transitions and keep the accuracy of the school figures. During the task the horse moves from lesson to lesson. The rider achieves this by preparing the horse at the right time with half-halts so that an energetic harmonious presentation is performed.

Walk

During the daily training and in the appropriate tests a medium walk is ridden. The horse steps out in rhythm without hurrying and overtracks with the hind legs over the footsteps of the front legs. If the hind legs do not overtrack those of the front, then the rider needs to go further forwards with the hands, allow the horse's neck to become longer and drive more with back and legs. It is advisable at walk to use the leg aids nearer to the girth. Throughout the rider should have a soft contact with the horse's mouth.

The canter.

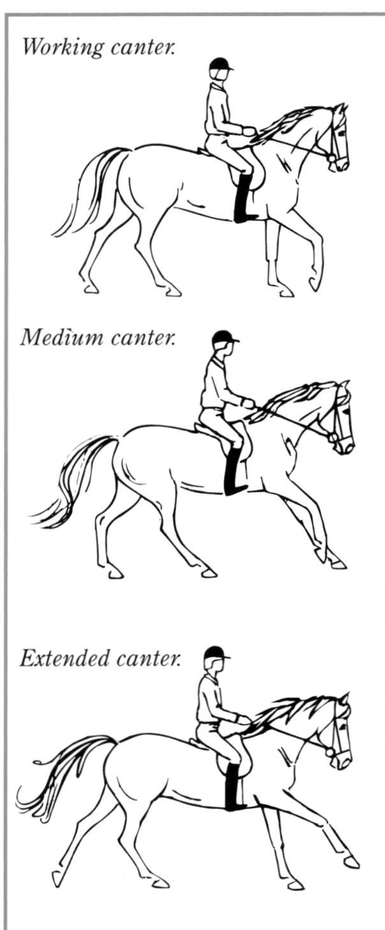

Trot

At trot there is a difference between the working and the medium. Before the changing from walk to trot the reins need to be firmer and the length must be continually corrected. The 'elastic band principle' and the flexible giving from the elbows makes a constant fine submission to the horse's mouth possible. During the working trot the horse moves in a regulated, swinging trot in good self-carriage. The horse's neck is firmly positioned out of the shoulder and is carried calmly. The horse moves with a visible forward impulsion. At the medium trot the tempo is increased and the horse must maintain the regular and equal rhythm. The medium trot is thus marked by energetic forward riding. The horse must not hurry but must step out energetically, stretching equally from both shoulders.

Canter

In the canter there is a difference between a working and a medium canter. The canter must not be executed with either any drag or hurrying of the pace but must be regular, swinging and in a clear, discernible three-time rhythm.

The working canter is characterised by a regular but energetic canter stride. The rider starts to drive without the horse hurrying. By stronger driving and simultaneously allowing extension to the canter strides in a clear three-time rhythm, the medium canter is achieved. Here the movements become longer and cover more ground, but the horse must not hurry and must remain under the application of the rider's aids. In the right canter the horse should be placed right and in the left canter towards the left.

We need to remind ourselves that the canter should be regulated and ridden with energy in a three-time rhythm. Horses often do not canter in balance with a regulated stride but seek to increase the pace whilst clearly supporting themselves on the rider's hand. A uniform canter rhythm should be the objective.

At walk, trot, and canter, the rider should at times remain passive with respect to his aids. In this way a regularity in the movement of the horse is established and balance is maintained.

Single Canter Change

If a change of rein is to be performed at canter only the simple change is required in the elementary tests. The horse is brought to a walk with the transition being carried through smoothly on a straight line. After one or two clear steps of walk, the canter is begun again. The rider should practise the transition to walk on a curved line (like an element of a circle). The introduction to the transition should only happen at the point where the horse canters calmly with a well-regulated stride, waiting, as it were, for the aid from the rider. This is easier to achieve on a curved line than when cantering on the straight. The well-executed transition will give the rider a sense of achievement: he should draw the horse into it, pat it and for the time being be content with what has been achieved.

The improvement of a particular lesson will be the aim in many hours practise. The rider should, however, stick to the methodical principles of learning and not too frequent, long periods of monotonous exercising which only cause resistance in the horse. An exercise should end with praise, even when it is not quite perfect.

Transitions

Transitions from one pace to another, or one tempo to another, should be clear, soft and easily discernible. Pace and tempo must remain clear until the completion of the exercise, the horse must remain light on the bit and with the correct position of the head.

Moving progressively through half halt to halt.

The Halt

In the transition to halt the forward movement should be soft and above all it should be arrested by the increased engagement of the hind legs. The halt should never be brought about by vigorous application of the rider's hand but must always be achieved softly, mainly by applying the legs and back. Afterward the horse must stand squarely and straight on all four legs. It must stand motionless for at least five seconds and remain light on the bit. Stepping backwards on the hind legs is a fault and a correction forwards is only a small mistake. The horse will become calm if the rider, breathing out consciously, has thoroughly relaxed hands and is loose in the shoulders.

Every lesson demanded in a dressage test finds expression as the result of a logical build up. The horse's halt, as with the other movements, falls into one of three forms. These are a basic form, a rough form and a fine form.

Basic form: the horse must learn to stand still for as long as the rider requires. Rough form: the horse must stand still and come up to the hand of the rider. Fine form: immobility – balanced outline with constant submission.

These terms of evaluation are also used in exercises involving other movements. For example in the volte:

Basic form: the rider is in the position to display a circle bend of approximately 10 steps diagonal.

Rough form: the horse remains constant on the rein and in rhythm.

Fine form: the horse is bent equally in the volte, remains on one track line and is continuously on the rider's aids.

Rein Back

In the lower grade tests the rein back asks for a movement to the rear equal to one length of the horse. In more advanced tests a certain number of steps are demanded. The rein back reveals the submission and obedience of the horse. It must be carried out willingly and equally on a straight line, without hesitating and without too much hurrying. The foot sequence follows a two-time rhythm as at trot and should be clearly recognisable. By moving backwards too quickly or creeping too slowly the horse evades the control of the rider's aids and no longer remains steady on the rein. The rein back is introduced by equal squeezing from both legs.

Prerequisite: relaxed standing on the rein, therefore a willing acceptance of the aids. Half-halts, given with both hands, bring about the backwards movement in a diagonal foot sequence. The measure of taking the rein aids, done concurrently with the

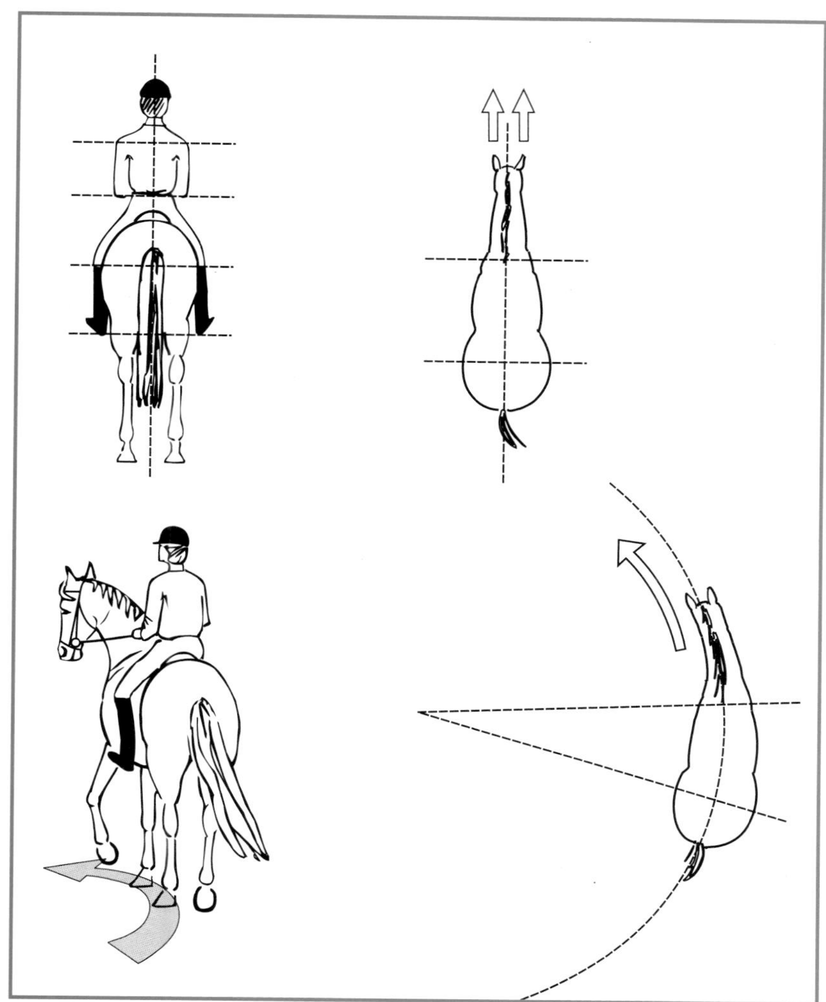

Horse and upright rider in balance, shoulders and hips in alignment. The 'straight' horse moves forward without the quarters deviating from the track of the forefeet: on the volte the track of the hindfeet follows that of the forefeet.

arresting back of the rider, produces the desired number of steps. To prevent crookedness, squeeze more strongly with the leg on the evading side.

Directional Changes

In the change of rein across the long diagonal, the horse turns six steps after the corner and joins the opposite track six steps before the opposite corner. The corners must be ridden on the track at a quarter of a circle. On the volte the horse with its full length must be positioned over the circle, which will be about six to eight steps diameter, and in this it must be bent in such a way that in an equal circle it shows only one hoofline.

When riding on the circle, the line of the circle must be kept. At half a horse length before each circle point the rider must reach the track, a half-horse length afterwards turn again and ride towards the next circle point. The horse will find itself continuously on a curved line and should never become straight.

If a change of the curved line is necessary, before reaching the new position the horse must be straightened for one horse length. In all turns the inner seat bone must be applied with more weight and care must be taken that the rider does not sit outwards and bend at the hips.

Lessons to Collection

More advanced tests are characterised by the collection of the horse at the trot and at the canter. At first only a low degree of collection is required. Now the sixth point in the training needs explanation, collection. In collection the horse must lower the quarters and shorten its base. It moves with elevated steps covering less ground and assumes an upright outline. The swing, however, must be retained and the hind legs must be engaged increasingly under the point of balance of horse and rider. This will mean that the quarters bear more weight and the forehand is lightened. The horse raises itself up, as it were, it gets bigger in front of the rider and the neck becomes the highest point. The term relative uprightness is used to mean that the uprightness is relative to the lowered quarters. A fault in the upright outline is known as total uprightness. It is not the result of actual collection but comes about by continuous half-halts by the rider. As a result of this, the activity in the back of the horse is reduced and engagement of the hind legs is prevented. This training error shows itself especially at the canter; the horses do not canter in a clean three-time but in a four-time rhythm. It is also possible for riders to allow the hand to predominate, a serious fault that results in no more than a retraction of the nose and a loss of suppleness and engagement in the back and behind the saddle.

Turn on the Quarters

Here the horse turns 180° on the quarters. The inside hind foot, however, should not remain fixed on the ground. The rider must introduce forward movement with forward driving aids. The outer leg must stimulate the horse to step sideways and to continue to do so for as long as it takes to reach the track again. In order to make it easier for the horse to maintain forward movement it is advisable at the beginning to ride the circle bend somewhat wider.

Because in the turn on the quarters a horse is being positioned into the direction of the movement the weight be placed more on the hind legs. Decisive is the co-ordination of the driving and the halting aids, as the horse has to stay soft on the bit with correct head carriage and move forwards. If the driving aids are too strong, then it will evade by stepping to the side and the circle will be too large. If the driving aids are insufficiently applied then it will stick in the turn with the hind feet planted to the ground. If the hand has too strong an effect, it will step sideways or backwards, both serious faults.

The Basic Characteristics

are trained through	training test
Looseness	
Rising trot Leg shifts Canter change – trot Ground grid work Lungeing Free jumping	rein given forward by the hand
Rhythm	
Natural step sequence of the basic paces (purity of the paces) Ground grid work Transitions Half-halts (regulating)	employing driving aids
Submission	
Tempo change Rein aids taking, giving, retaining, controlling	regular, constant, and soft contact to the mouth of the horse (elastic band principle)
Impulsion	
Tempo change Medium Trot and medium canter More definite effects	both hind legs thrust forward increasingly to carry the weight
Straightening	
Riding circles Riding of turns Tempo changes Forehand aligned to quarters	both hind legs carry the weight equally – the stride remains the same on curved as on straight lines
Collection	
Lungeing Tempo changes Transitions Half – full halts Counter canter Work in hand	quarters correctly engaged and used energetically

Harmony in Dressage

In recent years there has been a change of emphasis in the dressage training of horse and rider. Young, athletic riders have set new precedents. Lighter, better bred horses require to be ridden with greater finesse and sympathy. Riders still seek the instructor's help, which is essential, but many have learned to train their own horses rather than rely on a professional producer.

Pressure and force have no place in modern dressage. There has to be a genuine understanding of the nature of the horse and his needs for riders to achieve harmony and success.

The Rider

The First Work with the Horse

At the beginning of the young horse's training his physical and psychological development is incomplete. By nature the horse is good-natured and looks for the trust of man. For this reason the first concern must be to win his trust and keep it.

One single failure by a rider during the training, one thoughtless, undeserved rebuke as a result of loss of self-control can shake this trust and put into question the successful outcome of the training. Rough handling by a stable attendant can have the same effect.

A young horse in a headcollar fitted with a chain lead to give greater control.

as Instructor

When a horse is first stabled after being out at grass, the change to hard food must be gradual and the feeding carefully supervised. The horse should be led round the yard for a few days to get used to the new surroundings.

Often at the beginning of the training too little attention is paid to *leading, ground work* and *lungeing*, however, all three together are pre-requisites to the success of training without problems. Young horses can be led on a lunge cavesson and soon learn to stand still at a little distance away from the trainer. These early lunge lessons are the equivalent of the nursery school for children and like their human counterparts horses begin to acquire discipline as they learn the exercises. Lessons should always be in an enclosed space where distractions are unlikely to occur. The first lesson is for the horse to learn to stand still and again and again the horse is quietened with '*Haaalt*' or '*Staaand*' in an even, sonorous tone. This word must sink into its memory and the deep tone, encouraging trust, must remain the same throughout the training. This ability to control and calm the horse by the voice will pay long-lasting dividends.

Even if it takes three, four days, weeks or months, this lesson has to be taught and learnt. It will be found to be of as much benefit to the trainer as to the horse, for it is the first test of the former's character.

The next step is to lead the horse in hand at walk and trot and to practise the halt, getting the horse ever more accustomed to the voice and the quiet indications made with the whip.

If after these exercises, which demand concentration, you want to give the young horse time to run free as a reward, the hall or riding ground are equally suitable. One single failure on the part of an instructor because of an outburst of **impatience** or a loss of **self-control** will have severe consequences. There will follow a loss of trust in the instructor, and also in the place where it is training – and both will not be easy to remedy because they become firmly anchored experiences in the long-term memory.

Lungeing on a circle from the cavesson is never problematic as long as the leading has been understood. Instead of just going alongside the horse, the lunge is slowly, a little at a time, allowed to become longer and one walks alongside at an ever greater distance. If the instructor steps out a smaller circle with calm, large strides, then the horse will step out this still larger circle line correspondingly. It is important that the teacher acts as an example for the horse and does his job properly.

It cannot be expected that a young horse will tolerate his instructor's mistakes. Right from the beginning it will show its reactions, whether it understands what the instructor wants or not.

A lot of patience must be invested in these initial stages of the training, which will pay dividends over the whole training period. Most problems occur when at the beginning things are made to move too quickly and insufficient patience is displayed. The horse in those circumstances is not given sufficient time to understand and to digest what has been learned. If a good foundation of trust has been laid in the mind of the horse and if it hears again and again the trusted, sonorous tones of the reassuring voice it knows and it begins to accept the same calm clear sequence of movement of the trainer, then there will be no difficulty when beginning to ride, particularly if the trainer remains with the horse, or better still sits on the horse himself. Anyone who moves around thoughtlessly when handling a horse, or is nervous and hurried has much to learn. Once more, we can calm ourselves with breathing exercises if we begin to feel irritation.

The Lunge, Exercise and Method

As a general rule it is better to lunge off the nose of a lunge cavesson than from the bit. A snaffle can, however, be worn under the cavesson and side-reins can be attached from the bit rings to the body roller or saddle. The side-reins should be fitted loosely, their influence being no more than the weight of the rein. They can be shortened as the head-carriage improves but must never be used to impose an outline. Side-reins used in that way will only cause the horse to resist by stiffening and hollowing the back.

Initially, an assistant can lead the horse round the trainer, who himself must move in concentric circles. Gradually, as the horse begins to understand what is wanted and responds to the vocal command the assistant exerts less and less influence until control has passed entirely to the trainer.

The basis of the lunge work is concerned with the horse moving from the whip into the hand, the trainer always positioning himself in line with the horse's hip. The whip, held in the right hand on the circle left, is used in gentle, sweeping movements on the ground behind the horse to encourage him to go forward. The lunge hand maintains a light contact on a nearly taut rein. It leads the horse forward and it can also be used as a gentle restraint if the horse indulges in a little impetuous behaviour.

Should the horse fall inwards towards the trainer, the whip, pointed quietly at the shoulder, is used to push him out again. If the horse attempts to break away from the control imposed by whip and hand do not attempt to fight him. Instead, go with him, keeping the position opposite the hip, vibrating the rein and all the time talking soothingly to him.

Lunge equally from both sides. Horses find it easier to circle to the left and right-handed trainers find it easier to work to that direction, but continuous lungeing on one side instead of making the horse supple contributes very materially to making him stiff on the other.

The voice, above all, is the essential element in the lunge exercises. The tone is soft and deep when calming the horse and asking for transitions downwards from one gait to another. It is used in a sharper, rising note, with a little executive snap, when the opposite is required. Always use the same words and the same intonation.

Long-Reining

The work on the lunge can be extended by the use of the long reins, when the horse is driven from the bit by two reins. As when the horse is under saddle the outside rein is used in a governing, supportive role and the inside one indicates the direction of the movement. The presence of the trainer, somewhat behind his pupil, provides the forward driving aid.

In expert hands it is possible to obtain quite spectacular results in the improvement of the carriage and the balance and to inculcate obedience to the lightest of pressures on the bit.

Conversely, it can do more harm than good in less experienced hands, shortening the stride and inhibiting the freedom of movement.

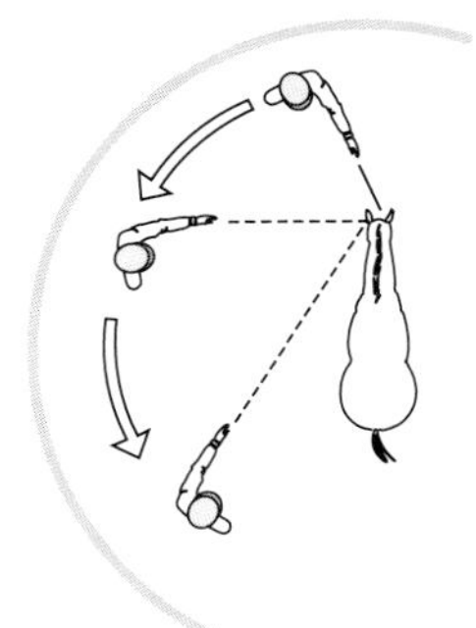

Preparatory to working the horse to the left, the trainer stands to the horse's front insisting on the horse remaining immobile. He then lengthens the rein and moves in a circle to his right,

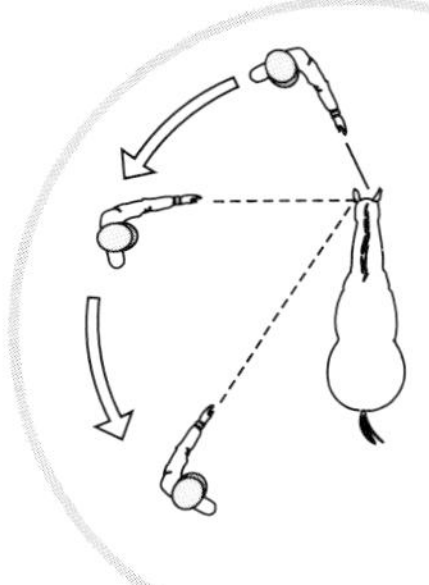

carrying the whip in his right hand. When the trainer is slightly behind the horse's hip he can encourage the horse to move forward and follow the track of the circle to the left.

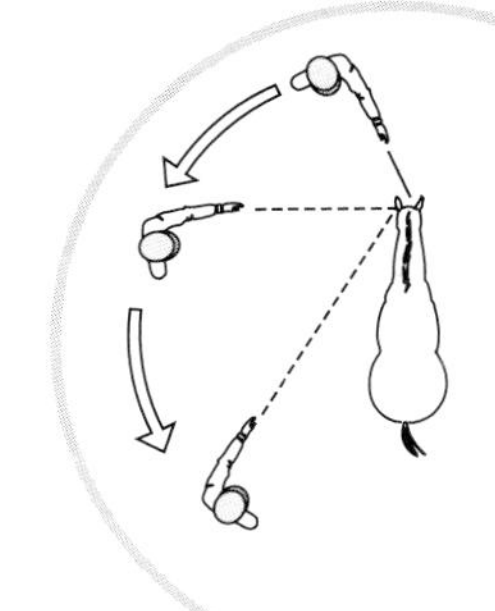

The rider working the horse downwards into a rounded back in the preparation phase of the training session.

a. The trainer correctly positioned to drive the horse forward from the whip into contact with the hand.
b. The whip used to prevent the shoulder from falling inwards.
c. The horse moving forward has taken up the slack of the lunge line.

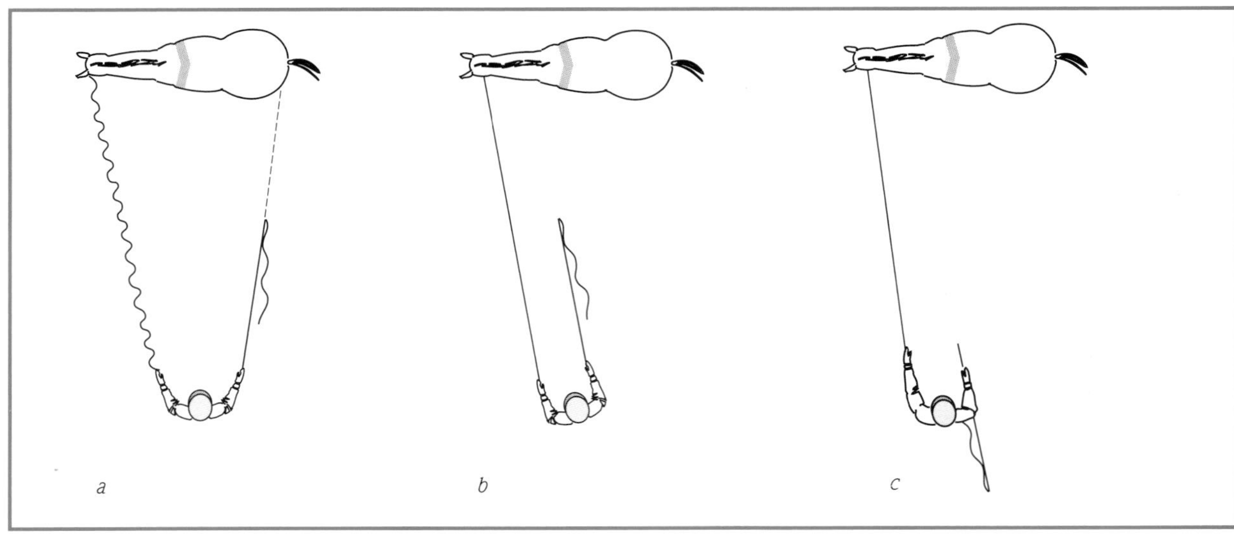

Teaching the piaffe in hand with the tactful use of the whip.

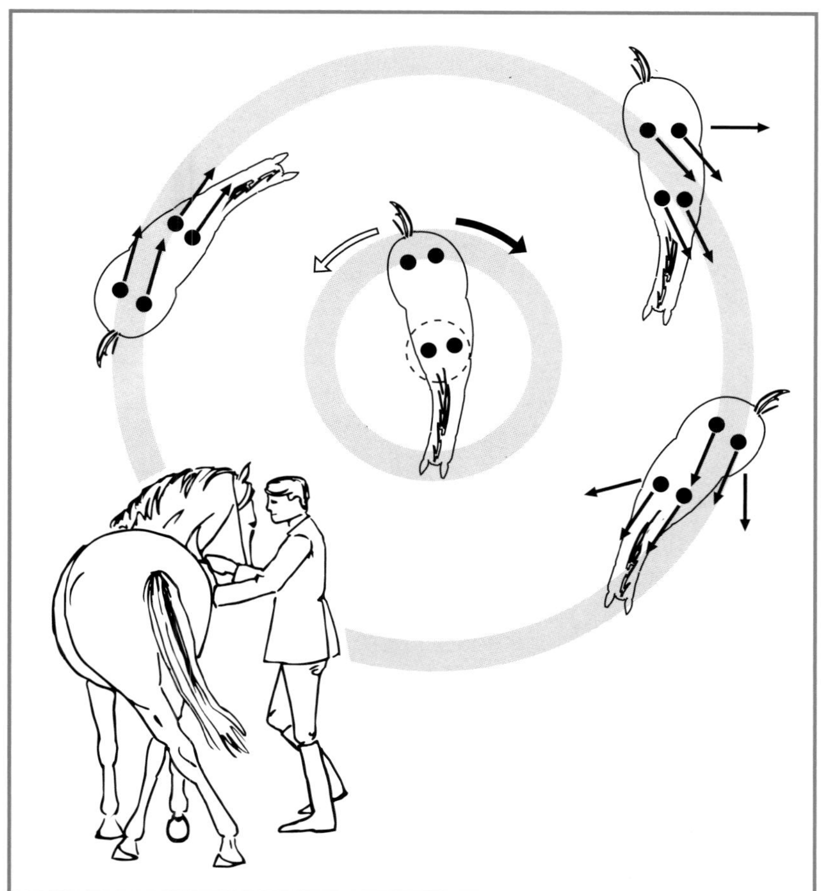

It is possible by judicious handling of the reins and the correct positioning of the body to teach the beginning of lateral work from the ground.

Riding Young Horses

The work on the lunge and long-reins will have gone some way toward preparing the horse physically and mentally to being ridden under saddle. Initially, the early riding of the young horse is directed, at first, to getting him to accept weight on his back and then learning how to carry it in balance.

The riding-in of young horses demands sensitivity and skill on the part of the rider and his assistants. When the horse has had sufficient preparation on the lunge it can be 'backed' by a quiet, experienced rider whilst an assistant holds the lunge rein. The horse is then urged to move quietly forward. After a few days on the lunge the horse can be ridden independently in the school area and then in the open in company with an older, steady horse. The riding sessions should never be so long that the horse becomes tired, for that is when he may be driven into making resistances.

The longer the period of lungeing and long-reining before the first ride the better. Once the horse is confirmed in forward movement the rider can establish a light constant contact with the mouth, but first only at the trot. At the walk the young horse should move free and unrestricted, almost without any contact to the mouth. Young horses must be encouraged to stretch their necks forward and down as part of each lesson. As a result of stretching the neck the back muscles benefit and are strengthened. Only then can the rider expect the horse to take his full weight. If one is talking about a real basis for the horse then this riding in depth beforehand will obviate almost all difficulties. Only this kind of training will lead to a true physical building up of a riding horse.

The First Exercises

When young horses can turn well and move with confidence on the circle, then they can be taught how to start to canter. This is easier for them to do on the left hand rather than on the right. The best time for this is when the horse has reached the closed side of the circle. With increased forward riding and driving with the inner leg, along with support of the voice, the rider can bring the horse to start to canter.

The proficient rider will feel when the inside hind leg is engaging under his seat bone at walk and trot and this is when cantering can begin.

The aids to start the canter are clear: the inner leg on the girth, the outer just behind the girth – this leg position, preceded by half-halts, will result in a clean canter stride so long as the leg squeezes at the optimum moment.

The Form of Exercise Sessions

The basic training includes the conditional development as well as the improvement of pace, balance, receptiveness and obedience. It should reveal to the experienced rider the potential and suitability of the horse for dressage, jumping or cross-country.

The daily exercise period is the smallest unit in the conditioning and training plan. Here a rhythm is built up that develops in the training over days, weeks, months and years.

This rhythm is subject to individual phases: Structure phase: basic training of the horse (ground work, cross-country, school).

Extension phase: learning new lessons at novice dressage levels; jump gymnastics; jumping single or multiple obstacles; special extension phases: perfecting particular movements; jumping a course of straightforward fences; canter training: jump training cross-country; experience of various ground conditions and unfamiliar obstacles.

Competition phase: confident jumping maintaining regular canter rhythm; increasing tempo; improving direction of line; active rest phase – ride in open terrain; maintaining training of performance and condition; lungeing/long-reining.

Format of a Training Session

The training period should be methodically constructed, nevertheless, it should be individually suited to the young horse.

Warming-up: achieve a looseness of horse and rider; working and test phases; learning new lessons; improvement of tasks already mastered; increasing performance capacity; testing performance level; relaxation phase, quiet finish; ride the horse dry; relaxation for horse and rider in open country.

The training of a horse must not be one-sided. With young horses it is a good idea to ride them once or twice a week in open countryside. Riding over undulating ground encourages looseness and relaxation; it develops balance, initiative and confirms forward movement.

Preparing for Dressage Competition

Good performances by both horse and rider can only be achieved after many years of systematic training. Building on the solid basic training of the horse, so that it can master the obedience, looseness and rhythm required for preliminary dressage tests, one can then begin training for more advanced work. A light degree of collection is achieved by a further development of the working trot, whereby the trot becomes more expressive and elevated. Frequent transitions from the medium trot to the working trot and the other way round stimulate the energy of the quarters. As a result of the change between stretching and bending the impulsion and carrying power of the hind legs gradually increases. At the beginning the collection should only be practised for short periods of time so that the horse is not driven into making evasions.

If the steps, for example, become flat and lose expression then what has to be improved first is back activity and submission through a more swinging, forward drive. If the horse lays itself on the hand in the collected tempo, then light

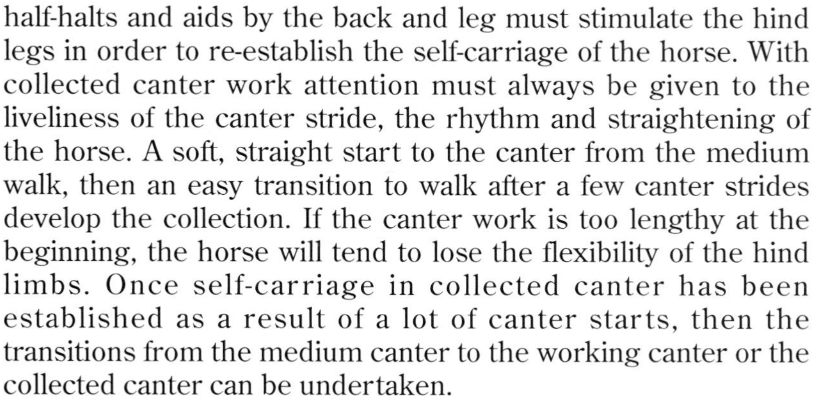

half-halts and aids by the back and leg must stimulate the hind legs in order to re-establish the self-carriage of the horse. With collected canter work attention must always be given to the liveliness of the canter stride, the rhythm and straightening of the horse. A soft, straight start to the canter from the medium walk, then an easy transition to walk after a few canter strides develop the collection. If the canter work is too lengthy at the beginning, the horse will tend to lose the flexibility of the hind limbs. Once self-carriage in collected canter has been established as a result of a lot of canter starts, then the transitions from the medium canter to the working canter or the collected canter can be undertaken.

Now the horse can be introduced to the counter canter. The easiest way to proceed with the counter canter is by riding a return volte after the second corner of the long side without changing the canter lead. After this the horse will be ridden through the curved corners in light collection in the counter canter. It is important that the rhythm and liveliness of the strides are retained. The rider should consciously remain seated on the same seat bone and make no move to change the lead by altering the body position. The horse remains positioned outwards in that bend and thus cannot change legs if the rider is correctly seated. When riding voltes care should be taken that the swing and the rhythm are retained. Attention must be paid to the elastic, springy action of the hind legs. The slow lengthening and shortening of the stride will develop the thrust and power of the hind legs. Any exaggeration in the rider's seat or aids will cause the horse to become confused.

Perfect control, perfect harmony and perfect poise.

The Training of

The length of time required to train a jumping horse will depend on the skill of the rider and the disposition of the horse for jumping.

A properly planned training programme can only be undertaken when the horse has absolute confidence in the rider. It must move forwards, begin to canter willingly and allow itself to be checked quietly. The dressage type schooling, however, must stand absolutely at the forefront. Next to ground grid work, young horses should first learn to cross one or more coloured poles on the ground. Then a few low fences at heights of 30-40cm approached from trot can be jumped. Jumping loose or on the lunge is also beneficial and improves the ability to measure the fences independently of the rider. To learn jumping with a rider must first be practised in the arena and then in the open. The temperament of the horse demands a skilful grading of the driving aids. In the case of horses that rush, the rider must sit calmly and work with a reassuring voice. An impetuous horse is best dealt with by being jumped out of trot, and only later being allowed to canter. These jumping exercises are done roughly twice a week. The exercises are directed at getting the horse to jump willingly and confidently and to increase its ability to measure distances. Even if the horse looks like becoming particularly talented the demands made upon it must be limited. A horse will only be a confident jumper when it has learned to cope with height by gradual stages. Horses lose the desire to jump if too much is asked of them, or if they are always jumped over the same obstacle. Even using the simplest of means, fences can be changed in appearance and it is always possible to make alterations in the track.

It is not essential to train with all those obstacles likely to be found in a competition. Most horses, once on the track will jump confidently for an experienced rider. When horses stiffen and lose their good shape over fences the fault is almost exclusively that of the rider unless there is some underlying physical discomfort. If injury is not the cause the rider must concentrate on flowing with the movement without disturbance or the need to drive more strongly.

A jump is executed in the canter, and so corrections can only be made in that pace. If a horse hesitates ('backs off') when jumping or refuses, then it will first be necessary to re-establish a regular good rhythm in the canter strides and the overall pace. Nothing can be done by way of correction over the actual

a Jumping Horse

fence. Proper preparation is the prerequisite for successful and harmonious jumping. If horses canter easily and regularly in quiet contact with the hand then they will also stretch out over small obstacles using a relaxed back. From a top grade jumper one expects sufficient jumping power to clear obstacles of the height and difficulty appropriate to the class and that ability cannot be allowed to deteriorate during the course of the competition.

Many horses, though they have the necessary qualities, do not jump well in competition because they are insufficiently supple and developed. One of the main objectives of the jumping training is to develop the jumping technique of the horse by a meaningful, natural progression (ground, grid work, jumping over fixed obstacles in the open country etc). Horse

This rider has moved his own centre of gravity as near to that of the horse as is possible to create a combined point that enables the horse to fully utilise its power.

Three riders and three horses, but single harmony. Compare the techniques of the horses. Balance and leg styles all differ.

The seats of the riders are, however, all in harmonic tune with the horses. The expressions on the faces of all competitors show concentration and determination.

and rider should also form a unit when jumping. The horse needs to be supple, strong and athletic but so does the rider. He, like his horse, must work at specific gymnastic exercises leading to greater flexibility in the joints and improved athleticism. The half-seat, the jumping position, demands great suppleness if the rider is to be as one with his horse. In addition a good jumping rider will be quick in his reactions and tactically good in competition. The training of the horse includes the maintenance and improvement of the good basic schooling achieved by work on the flat, and one must concentrate continually on increasing suppleness, encouraging the engagement of the hind legs and perfecting the paces. When taking part in competitions the strain on a jumping horse is much greater than during the usual training at home and so we must train to improve stamina and endurance sufficiently to meet the requirements of long, galloping courses over a number of fences that call for the expenditure of high levels of energy and effort. This sort of training can be undertaken in open country where ground conditions are good.

The development of jumping power is related directly to dressage riding which builds up muscles correctly and increases the strength and weight-carrying capacity of the hind limbs. Strength is also built up by making intelligent use of hills which can be ascended at a steady trot. These exercises are also recommended with ground grids 3.00-3.50m in front of a jump, ride forward in trot and jump from that gait. The obstacles for jumping out of the trot need only to be 0.50-1.10m.

In gymnastic jumping an increase to a height of over 1.10m is possible. Several obstacles set up one after each other, beginning with a low height, slowly increasing, are especially suitable for developing the jumping rhythm and technique and for improving the jumping power.

The distances between the obstacles are arranged to suit the stage of training and the length of the canter stride. Good gymnastic jumping leads easily to coping with double obstacles. At the same time the rider is learning to work actively or passively on the horse. The regular rhythm is actually forced upon the horse because of the distances between the obstacles and this helps the rider to get the feel for the right tempo.

Preparing for Competition

Working the horse in the collecting ring before entering the jump arena is of great importance. Sufficient time must be given to warming up so as to get rid of the natural tensions. Only then should the rider attempt some trial fences. As the obstacles always consist only of poles, one should begin with a low fence and not exceed the height demanded in the actual competition.

Every jumping rider should: Take sufficient time for working in (no hurrying); take pains to warm up sufficiently and be certain of the line he intends to take over the course, that means walking the course very carefully before the competition.

The bascule *over the fence and the leg technique are perfect.*

A perfect stretch over the water jump.

Demonstrating perfect positioning over a solid cross-country obstacle, this rider has the whip in his right hand, ready for a tap on the horse's shoulder, if required, without moving his hand position.

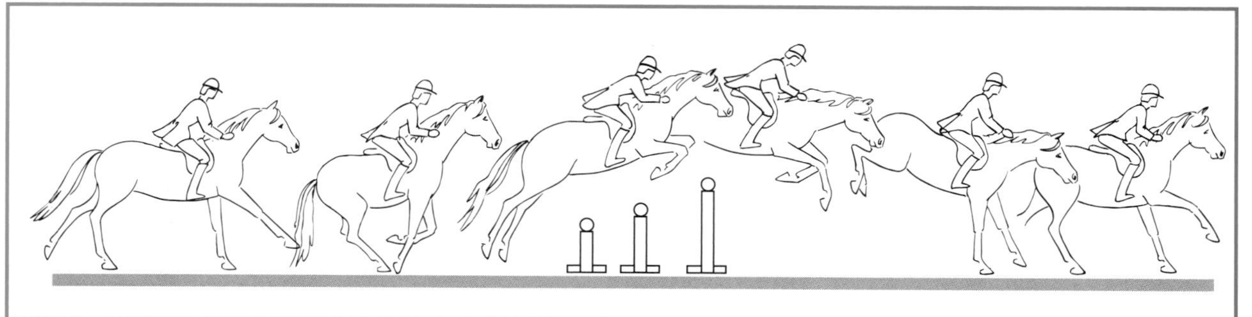

Anticipation and concentration before the jump.

Correcting Spoilt Horses

Correction always takes time and patience but will be made easier if the causes of the mistake have already been established. Under a good rider, able to apply the aids effectively, horses will usually pretty soon give up their bad habits, although the same problems may occur under a weak rider. Clumsiness, ignorance, bad riding and unfair punishment will certainly produce a spoilt horse. Conversely too much spoiling – usually from a false sense of love of animals – as well as weak handling can lead to bad habits.

Shying

If a horse shies away from an unknown object, one then attempts to ride it in the shoulder-in movement towards the object, and in such a way that the quarters are positioned more towards it. In the company of other horses a confident horse that does not shy should go first, the young horse will then willingly follow. It is important that the horse trusts the rider and can be calmed with the voice. The rider must under no circumstances show any insecurity or fear. In the case of temperamental horses one must keep calm.

Rearing

Should a horse resist by rearing, the rider must lean forward energetically. Rearing is the most dangerous of all bad habits and can only be corrected by a proficient rider and then only on soft and not on hard ground. The horse rears when it is allowed to stop and from the first sign one should ride forwards. In the long term this dangerous habit can only be remedied by energetic driving forward.

Group Allegiance

When horses are reluctant to leave a group it reflects the natural herding instinct *and* a lack of training. By using stronger aids of the back and legs, backed up by the whip, if necessary, this habit can be eliminated.

Bolting

A confirmed bolter is often difficult in temperament and not an easy ride, but normally well-mannered animals may bolt through fear and from what they imagine to be a dangerous situation. In this last instance a calm rider with a firm seat may be able to reassure the animal with his voice and, more practically, by turning the horse in a large circle.

On strong-pulling horses the temptation to use more severe bits should be resisted. A soft, thick mouthpiece, that does not cause pain, is more likely to result in success.

Tongue Defects

Badly fitting bits, particularly those that are too large or are adjusted too low in the mouth give encouragement to tongue problems. To avoid discomfort the horse can pull the tongue back and lay it over the bit, when the horse becomes out of the rider's control. However, tongue problems of this sort can also occur as a result of particular mouth formations and in such cases some form of mechanical restraint may be necessary.

Head Shaking

Shaking the head can be prevented by using a martingale for a time. It should be adjusted tight enough to be effective when shaking becomes violent. The simultaneous application of a half-halt – and this is important – along with an energetic driving will have the effect of stopping the bad habit after a short time. Head shaking may also be the result of a bridle that presses against the back of the ears because the browband is too short.

Boring

Horses that bore down against the rider's hand can be helped with half-halts accompanied by strong driving action. A cure can be affected by a competent rider.

Above the Bit

Unless there is some severe physical malformation the usual cause for horses to poke the nose upwards and carry the mouth above the hand is the 'upside-down' conformation produced by poor schooling and bad riding. Muscle is developed on the underside of the neck, the back is hollowed and, in consequence, the hind legs are unable to engage. The solution is to return to basics and work towards a rounded top-line by using poles and grids to encourage the neck to stretch down and forward. Educated riding will thereafter cure the problem, but it takes time.

Nervous Horses

Nervous horses require a calm, patient rider who will calm them by continual reassurance. Quiet hacking in the countryside involving long walking periods will be helpful, but it is with the character of the rider that any significant improvement will be achieved.

Jogging

As a result of nervousness or as the result of an acquired habit, horses will jog when out riding. The rider must continually arrest his horse, go forward with the hand and free the neck. Gradually, it will get into the habit to take free and longer steps. Calm with the voice and encourage the long-striding, free walk.

Pacing

A horse that paces (i.e. moves the legs in lateral pairs) can be prevented by continual walking on a long rein over undulating country and, in particular, up and down hills.

Lazy Horses

The lazy horse requires a firm but not rough rider and will go better in company than alone. A season's hunting will do wonders for horses of this sort and an increase in the ration of high energy feeds will not go amiss. Horses may naturally be of a lazy disposition, but often become lazy by being soured by over-schooling.

Bucking

Bucking is generally an expression of zest for life. If a horse has not jumped for some time, young as well as older horses may put in a buck after the first fence. An over-fresh horse, short of exercise, may also release its surplus energy by bucking. Horsemen should accept the occasional buck as a display of high spirits.

Persistent buckers are another matter. As a matter of course riders should examine the back and also the saddle-fitting. Otherwise strong, driving legs are necessary to send the horse forward and the hand should prevent the horse getting its head down. Horses that are short of exercise are best worked on the lunge before being ridden.

Running Out

Running out to one side or the other at a fence can be the result of overfacing the horse, a wrong approach, lack of basic training or, indeed, inexperience and lack of determination on the part of the rider. The remedies are obvious.

Refusals

Horses refuse for much the same reasons as they run out. Over-jumping so that the horse becomes soured is a common reason for refusals as, of course, is the fear of pain. If it hurts to jump because of some physical condition or because the horse is frightened of being pulled in the mouth by an incompetent rider, then, very sensibly, it stops. Those factors apart, horses that have gone sour or lost their confidence will often regain their enthusiasm by going hunting.

Jumping Hollow

A horse will hollow the back over a fence if it is jabbed in the mouth or if it anticipates such treatment. Otherwise it is the result of inexpert schooling – Back to Basics.

Some ways of increasing the horse's confidence and his acceptance of the unusual.

The Sport of Eventing

An air of confidence!

The sport of eventing is considered to be the ultimate test of horse and rider, both of whom must perform very competently in the dressage arena, over a steeplechase course and a demanding cross-country test before the final arena jumping.

The sport demands a horse of outstanding ability and a rider of similar quality. Whilst the dressage test is less complex than the Grand Prix for dressage horses, for instance, it has to be ridden with accuracy and lightness within the confined space of an arena on a horse that is fit enough to run for his life and still has to display obedience and submission to the rider.

The second day tests the horse's speed and endurance, as well as the courage of both partners over a steeplechase ridden at racing speed, a section of roads and tracks and a formidable cross-country course over fixed obstacles, water complexes and natural hazards.

Relaxed but alert.

An impressive jump over a drop fence. The rider inclines the body to the rear so as to cope with the steep descent but remains in balance and in control.

The horse has then to be 'fit for service' on the third day, when he and his rider have to negotiate a course of coloured show jumps in the arena. The course is not big by showjumping standards, nor does it involve difficult distances, but it represents a severe test after the exertions of the previous day. Furthermore, horse and rider have to adapt to the showjumping technique, which is very different to that employed over fixed cross-country obstacles taken sometimes at speed.

Without any doubt, the big, galloping Thoroughbred or near-Thoroughbred is the best, perhaps the only, horse for this supreme test of courage and physical ability.

Nonetheless, correct basic training in dressage, showjumping, gymnastic exercises etc. are absolutely vital to the eventer. Cross-country experience, after an introduction over straight forward schooling courses and a variety of fences, will be gained by competing in the progression that begins with pre-novice, one-day events, jumping with dressage competitions etc.

Interestingly, there is a gulf fixed between the one-day event and the full-blown three-day affair. It does not by any means follow that the good, or even the brilliant, one-day eventer will perform as well when faced with the problems involved in a test extending over three days.

A moment of mutual congratulation after the successful completion of the dressage test.

Hunting

The sport of hunting is still carried on enthusiastically in the traditional strongholds of Britain and Ireland, and still, indeed, supports a sizeable industry. In Britain alone over 60,000 people hunt every week during the fox-hunting season which begins on November 1 and continues into late April and May, having been preceded in September and October by cub-hunting which introduces young hounds to the business of the chase and also provides useful experience for young horses. In the summer months there is stag-hunting in Britain's West Country.

Hunting, based on the British pattern, is also well established in America, Australia and New Zealand.

A kind of hunting goes on in some of the countries of the European mainland, and France, in particular, has its own formalised, almost ritualistic type of hunting in pursuit of both boar and stag. However, the sport cannot be compared with that enjoyed in the British and Irish hunting countries where hunt followers ride in the wake of hounds over natural country and natural obstacles. Increasingly, there are 'hunt jumps' built in wire fences, for instance, but essentially the sport is about 'riding to hounds' come what may and over whatever country may present itself.

Of course, hunting is a sport in its own right and many horses are kept up solely for that purpose, but it can also provide a useful training ground for the competition horse.

Hunting is the ideal antidote for the horse that has gone stale through too much disciplined school work. For the young horse it develops endurance and stamina and it encourages the horse to use its own initiative. A good hunter soon acquires a 'cleverness' in negotiating obstacles and the varied terrain, including in some countries steep hills and wild moorland areas contributes wonderfully to a natural balance. It has, indeed, been said that a day's hunting does more for the balance of horse and rider than a week inside a schooling arena.

Two riders tackling a typical timber fence with enthusiasm.

Hunting is enormously enjoyable for both horses and riders and calls for a high degree of understanding between the two. Sometimes the rider can help his horse but just as often it is the good horse that gets his rider out of trouble. The relationship is just as close and harmonious as that required in the competitive disciplines, but without the tension that must inevitably accompany those pursuits.

For the event horse the background of hunting represents the best possible training opportunities.

Western Riding

Western riding has its origins in the centuries-old horse culture of the Iberian Peninsula taken to the New World by the *conquistadores* of the 16th century.

They took, also, their saddles and their unique system of bridling, both of which survive, allowing for adaptation to the saddle, in the art of the modern Californian reinsman.

Indeed, the school of Western horsemanship is just as legitimate as that of the 'classical' schools of Europe and requires just as much skill, dedication and devotion to basic training principles.

The two schools have as common objectives: lightness, obedience, relaxation in movement and the maintenance of a fluid balance.

The difference is one of purpose. The European dressage horse is trained for the tests involved in competition and performed in an arena of prescribed size, whilst the progressive exercises and movements have as their goal a state of high collection. Throughout the training the aim is to place the horse

The Western horse has to be very responsive and obedient as well as level-headed.

A highly-schooled cutting horse works the cattle instinctively on a 'floating' rein.

continually under the control of the rider, each movement made being dependent on the will of the latter and upon the application of his aids. The situation by no means precludes the harmonious interplay between the two but the horse has, of necessity, to be entirely subordinate to the rider. However willing and co-operative the animal's individuality is expressed only in the manner in which it carries out the command given by the rider; the horse itself is never responsible for initiating any of the movements that comprise the performance.

The dressage rider uses a mix of more or less continual driving and halting aids to maintain rhythm and secure the engagement of the hind legs. He makes use, also, of the double bridle, employing both hands.

Conversely, the training of the Western horse has the practical objective of producing a working horse, primarily for the purpose of handling cattle, and the movements, unlike those of the dressage horse, are carried out at speed – dressage at the gallop, in fact. The Western training encourages a free self-carriage with minimal rein influence (the aim of the classical schools of the Reformation period) and whilst the hind legs are still required to provide the propulsive thrust the outline is more extended, with the head and neck being similarly stretched, although the horse will be well able to 'tuck in' when asked to rein-back, for instance. Nevertheless, in reining classes just as much emphasis is put on the purity of the three gaits – the walk, jog and lope – as is given to the dressage equivalents. Spins, or pivots (pirouettes at speed) the roll-backs and the spectacular sliding halts are movements essential to the working of cattle.

Perhaps the line of demarcation between the two is most strongly marked by the degree of independent action allowed to the horse. In dressage, the horse is dependent throughout on the rider. The Western horse, on the other hand, is encouraged to develop and act on his own initiative when working cattle.

The highly-schooled cutting horse, for example, works instinctively and separates the calves in almost the same way as a sheepdog moves sheep, responding to no more than minimal indications made by the rider.

The Western saddle is to all intents a work-platform and whilst the leg has an obvious use, the Western rider's aids are much concerned with the use of the weight – a highly developed factor in Western horsemanship.

Furthermore, the Western horse is bridled and mouthed through the hackamore system involving a progression of *bosal* (noseband) which begins with a very heavy one, finely balanced so that it touches neither nose nor chin so long as the head is carried acceptably, and ending with a pencil-thin *bosal* that

The sliding stop – an immediate halt from the canter.

serves only as 'a reminder'. When the hand is raised a momentary restraint is applied to the nose encouraging the horse to 'tuck in', i.e. retract the nose. The *bosal* acts similarly should the head be raised above the acceptable limit.

The heel knot, at the back of the *bosal,* which lies between the jawbones, acts in opposition to prevent overbending and to discourage evasion of the nose contact, when that is brought into play.

Fitted and used by an expert this is a precision instrument capable of a fine adjustment quite beyond the conventional European bridle.

The completion of the bridling process and its ultimate refinement is the transition to the fearsome, high-ported, long-cheeked spade curb bit. By then the horse has been, as it were, mouthed through the nose, and the bit, in the hands of the expert, exerts only the lightest pressure on the mouth. Indeed, the finished horse performs on no more than the weight of a floating rein – the very apotheosis, one might think, of the 'classical' tradition.

(It is interesting to note that the classicism of the Reformation and, indeed, equestrian practice up to and beyond the 18th century employed a similar system of bitting using the clumsier combination of cavesson and *cereta,* the studded Spanish noseband, with the bit to obtain a head-carriage depending upon minimal rein contact.)

The Western horseman rides with one hand and neck-reins with an appropriate shift of the body weight to indicate the required changes of direction.

At the highest level Western horsemanship exemplifies a near-ultimate harmony between horse and man.

An example of easy, flowing balance with the horse being ridden in a bosal *acting lightly on the nose.*

Western training involves gymnastic exercises carried out at speed and demands great suppleness and balance. This young horse is ridden in the hackamore bosal.

FURTHER

SCHOOLING

The ability to achieve mutual harmony creates the potential for success.

Lateral Movements

The use of lateral movements within the gymnastic exercises serves to make the horse more agile and supple. Riding lateral movements can only be begun when the horse has learned from the work on the circle and the volte, to engage the inner hind leg more strongly. The carrying out of lateral movements at the walk only serve at the beginning as a means of becoming more familiar with the movement and of refining the aids. A gymnastic value is not attained.

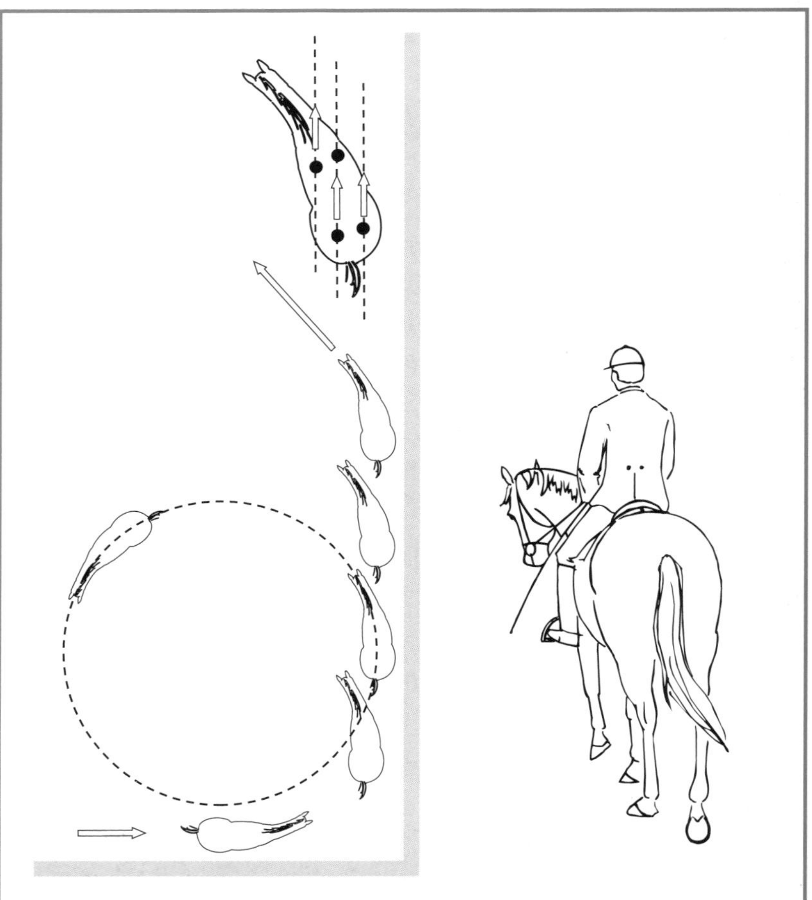

Shoulder-in approached from a correct bend on the circle.

Shoulder Fore

Starting point for lateral movements is the shoulder fore on a single track. What is meant by this is that in the case of horses having already a light degree of collection, only a limited positioning away from the wall is required.

The horse moves on the long side of the arena with the inner hind leg tracking between the line made by the forefeet. The outer hind leg follows the track of the outside forefeet. A curvature that goes evenly along the whole length of the horse inwards is just about visible. This is lost if the outer hind leg deviates towards the outside. The execution and aids are the same as with the following shoulder-in but are adjusted to produce a slight degree of bend through the body. The development of the shoulder fore is best carried out after riding through the first corner on the long side. To maintain the bend through the corner, the fore hand is led with both reins on the inner edge of the school track. The inner rein maintains the bend, the outer rein governs the bend and regulates the tempo. The inner leg behind the girth produces the bend in the ribs, stimulates the inside hind leg into active engagement and, in connection with the outer rein, causes the horse to move sideways. In part, the outer leg both controls and drives to prevent deviation of the quarters. The rider adjusts the sitting position to the bend, the hips being in line with those of the horse.

Shoulder In

The shoulder in, the basic position from which all other lateral movements are developed, requires a further increase in the curvature and an increased movement of the fore hand away from the track. As a result the horse moves on a broadened track. Now it moves forwards with the head positioned away from the movement with the inside feet treading in front of the outer and the outer shoulder positioned a little in front of the inside hip. The balance of the rider rests more on the inside seat-bone. At the beginning the rider should be satisfied with just a few steps and should then move straight forward again.

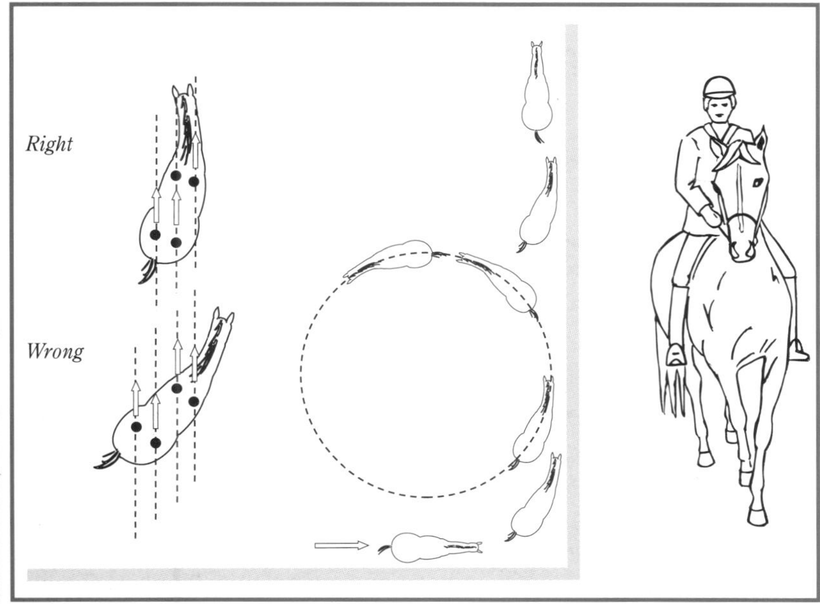

The correct degree of bend on three tracks and the opposite four-track movement.

The shoulder in can also be executed on the centre line and is in any event performed to either hand.

Faults and Correction:
The main mistake is to use the inner rein too strongly. This results in too much bend in the neck causing the outside shoulder to fall outwards. To counteract this fault the outer rein is used in conjunction with a driving outside leg.

Travers

Travers (head to the wall or quarters-in) is a lateral movement in which the quarters are positioned towards the inside and the horse is bent in the direction of the movement. The track of the hind legs lying towards the inside of the arena is at least half a step away from the track of the outside foreleg. The outer leg step forwards and sideways over the inner.

Execution and Aids: Before the transition to travers it is necessary to bring the horse to collection and to keep the rhythm by more forward driving aids. As soon as the rider has ridden deep into the corner with the head almost at the long side, he executes a half-halt and begins the travers. The outer

Exercises on the circle leading to half-pass to the left with the head held correctly in the direction of the movement.

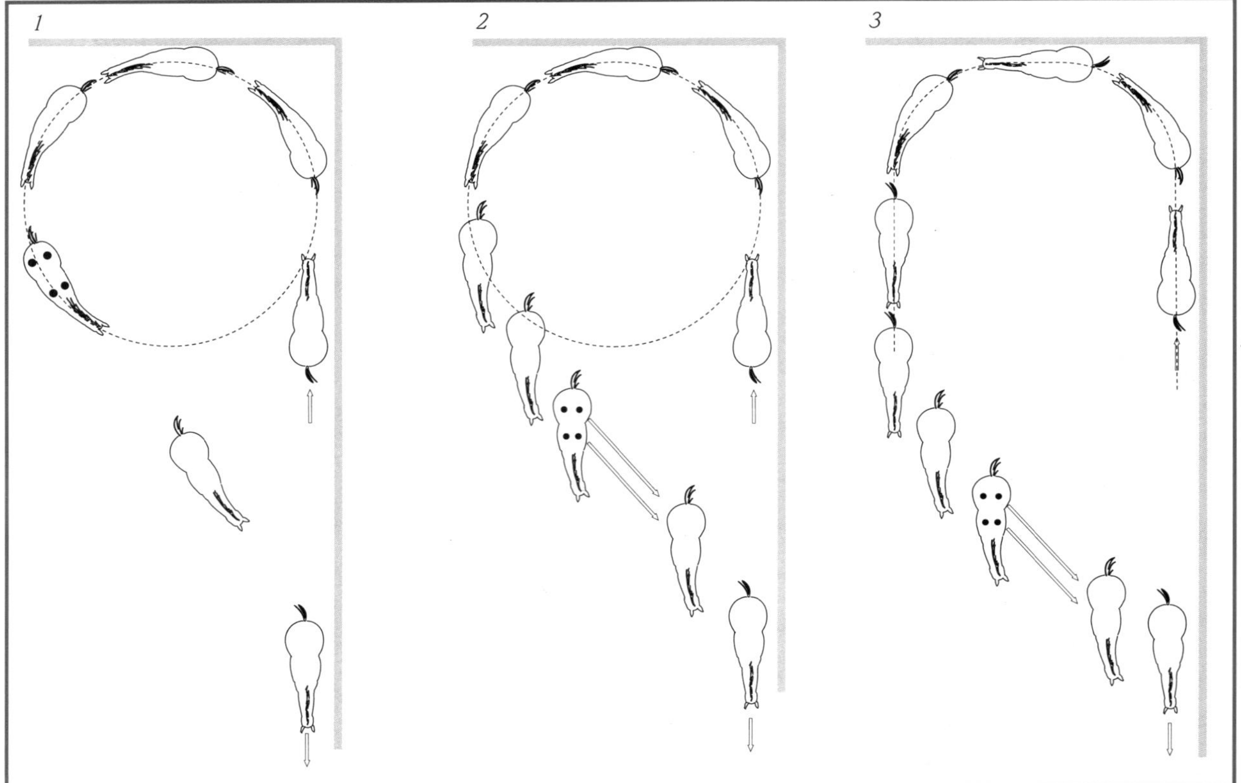

leg is pressed flat against the horse and behind the girth, the inside leg holds the bend, maintains the forward movement and acts otherwise as in shoulder-in. The outside hand predominates and acts in concert with the inside leg.

The important points are: In the transition to travers the horse is brought to collection; the neck of the horse must also be appropriately bent from the shoulders; the outer leg lies behind the girth and obtains, together with the inner rein, the sideways movement of the horse.

Faults and correction: A main fault in travers is for the horse to be bent largely at the shoulder instead of through the whole neck and body. The outside hind leg will then go further to the side than forwards and as a result the bend becomes false. The increased use of the inner leg and the outer rein will establish the correct curvature again.

Half-pass to the left. Well crossed legs and good balance of both horse and rider.

Half-pass to the right in perfect balance.

Renvers

Renvers, which is the opposite to travers, offers the same advantages in the training as the travers and shoulder-in but is a more difficult exercise. In this lateral movement the fore hand of the horse is positioned into the arena inwards, hence tail-to-the-wall or quarters out.

Execution and aids: The renvers position is obtained by the outer leg driving sideways, in co-operation with the inner rein, to produce a bend around the inner leg, which then immediately drives forwards. The outer rein lying on the horse's neck determines the degree of the bend and regulates the tempo.

Faults and correction: If the inner leg drives too strongly, then the horse will come too heavily on the hand. Too long and too much practise of the lateral movements minimises the swing of the horse. If a horse resists the aids or starts to canter, then the shoulder-in should be ridden until the horse comes to trot and can be prepared anew for the appropriate lateral pace.

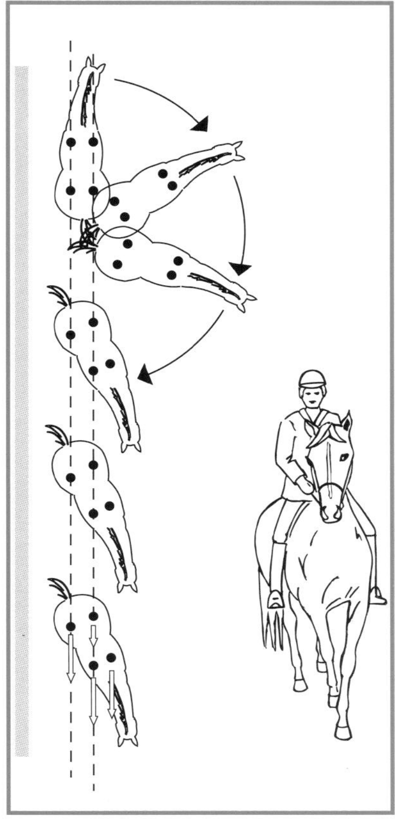

The turn on the quarters employed to obtain the renvers *movement, known as tail-to-the-wall or quarters out.*

Half-Pass

In half-pass the horse moves forward obliquely, slightly bent round the rider's inside leg and with head inclined in the direction of the movement. The movement frees the shoulder and consolidates the balance. In its development and execution the basic rule applies: pace, posture, bend.

Execution and aids: Half-passes can be ridden at walk, trot and canter and are approached from the circle with the object of moving forwards and sideways with the horse's body as nearly as possible parallel to the long side. The outside legs pass and cross over the inside ones. The rider's weight is held on the inside seat bone, the inside hand opens a shade to direct the movement, the outside rein supports by being on the neck. The outside leg acts flat behind the girth to push both forwards and sideways, the inside leg acts on the girth to sustain the movement.

Faults and correction: An exaggerated position of the head obstructs the free, springy pace and leads to rhythm faults, lack of collection and bend. If the rider bends in the hips and sits against the direction of movement, a mistake sometimes made by young riders, the horse becomes out of balance.

Flying Canter Change

In a flying canter change, which is required in the most advanced tests, the horse must change the canter in the air, i.e. jump from right to left lead and vice-versa. As the canter is a continued series of strides in three-time rhythm and the phases are made up of touch-down and suspension the change can only take place during the suspension phase.

The change must always be made in full forward movement, without deviating from the line.

The easier change is from the right into the left canter lead. From a volte in canter the horse is ridden in a slightly travers position in the direction of the track. After a few canter strides in right canter the rider, using his outer seat bone pushes the horse toward the inside of the arena in a sideways-forwards direction.

Whilst doing so the right leg is taken behind the girth and with the co-operation of leg and hips the jump over is achieved. Even with an immediate success the exercise should be discontinued, it is best to take a short rest at the walk with loose reins. Lots of praise is important!

In the next few weeks of training this change needs to be consolidated and only then can the change to the right rein begin and the movements gradually refined. Experienced riders only begin the flying changes when the horse is sufficiently schooled and strong enough for the exercise. The preparation begins with making frequent canter starts from the walk on both leads. Beginning to canter from the walk and the transition from the canter to the walk must be executed without any trotting steps. In the counter canter the rider has the means to prepare for the first flying change.

Execution and aids: The aids are taken in exactly the same way as for the beginning of canter on one lead or the other. From the counter canter to the canter on the inside lead the inner leg is positioned on the girth, the outer comes behind the girth. The head is positioned slightly inwards and the weight of the rider moved from outside to inside. The inner leg, lying on the girth, asks for the flying canter change in suspension. All these aids take place simultaneously.

Faults and correction: Horses may change first in front and then at the rear or may not come through completely with the hind legs. In such instances it is the canter pace that must be improved before changes are attempted. Pronounced crookedness in the changes is corrected by stronger more active forward movement. One can only begin with the flying change in several tempi when a horse has mastered the single flying change. The change will only be successful and smooth

Flying canter change to the left. This phase, with a single leg support is difficult to observe by eye.

when the rhythm of the canter is maintained in easy collection and is as regular and set as a clockwork mechanism.

Pirouette

The pirouette counts as one of the most difficult exercises. In the pirouette (half turn: 180° or complete turn: 360°) the horse makes the turn in three to four strides for the half-pirouette and six to eight for the full pirouette. The horse turns in canter rhythm on the pivot of the inside hind leg. It is taught out of the travers or renvers position or can be developed from half-pass.

Pirouette to the left. The muscles in the neck of the horse are clearly visible.

Execution and aids: In the pirouette the inner rein leads the horse in the turn. The inner leg placed on the girth encourages the movement and prevents a falling in of the horse over the inner shoulder. The outer leg, supported by the outside rein, is put on behind the girth to hold the quarters. The outer rein must, however, allow the movement to the inside, for the horse should be bent and positioned inwards. The rider moves his weight more onto the inner seat bone and maintains on upright upper body.

Faults and correction: If the quarters are not held in position the pirouette will become no more than a volte or a turn on the centre. The horse has to jump into pirouette and can only do so as a result of cantering forwards in a strong medium canter. Only when this is established can pirouette be attempted.

The rider working with the trainer, the latter acting as 'the mirror on the ground'.

Piaffe

The piaffe is a rhythmic, elevated, trot executed on the spot, or more correctly, with just a little gaining of ground to the front. The tips of the hoof of the fore foot is raised in line with the middle of the cannon bone of the opposite limb. The lifted hind foot rises in line or just above the fetlock of the opposite leg. Perfect balance, a continuous urge forwards and great activity are the basis of a regular rhythm sequence in the piaffe.

Execution and aids: At the beginning of the training in the piaffe under the rider supple and soft transitions to increased collection are required. Changes of tempo at trot on the long wall are practised with the object of reducing more and more the gaining of ground to the front and increasing the elevation of the gait.

After the first successful, considerably shortened steps are obtained the horse must be returned into the collected trot. The rider in introducing the piaffe must sit more deeply in the saddle and by bracing the back strengthen the pressure on the back of the horse. The horse must now, as a result of the weight and the gentle squeeze of the leg, increasingly go onto the bit. The leg aids applied to the girth should drive the horse forwards in order to keep the lively engagement of the hind legs well beneath the body.

Faults and correction: Over use of the whip leads inevitably to tension and resistance. The result will be hurried, irregular steps and a stiffening of the back. Where horses are over-ridden or do not have the ability to flex the hind legs sufficiently, the lowering of the croup is prevented and the hind feet

Piaffe on the long reins making use of a roller fitted with appropriately positioned rings.

Piaffe – dancing harmony.

hardly lift off the ground. The correcting aids must always encourage the swing, and the seat and aids should permit a little movement forwards before re-adjusting the movement so that the horse advances by only a few centimetres at a time.

Passage

The passage is a suspended, elevated trot in which the horse maintains a rhythmical movement forwards instead of gaining little or no ground as in piaffe.

Execution and aids: The passage can be taught from the piaffe, from trot or from the walk. If a horse has learned a precise piaffe, then the passage can be developed from the piaffe. If teaching the passage from the trot, then it is taught in tempo change each following shortly upon the other. The quick halting and driving aids following each other will cause the horse to make a few suspended steps. In the passage the same aids are given as for the trot. A light hand, a supple upright seat with a more strongly braced back, coupled with an increased activity of the legs encourage the elevation of the steps. The supporting whip aids applied from the ground are applied upwards and just behind the rider's leg. Real artists applying these aids obtain astounding results. Touching is something anyone can do, but to know where, how, and when it should be done – that is the art.

Faults and correction: A passage is faulty when the hind legs are dragged and show no lift. More frequently, however the elevation behind is uneven because the horse is either crooked or the legs of the rider are not evenly effective on each side. The best cure is always to ride the horse for a time allowing for a greater gain of ground to each stride.

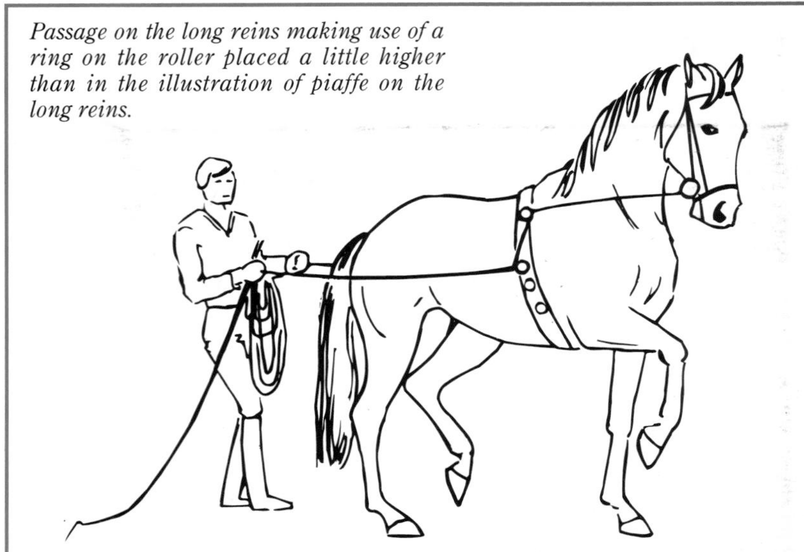

Passage on the long reins making use of a ring on the roller placed a little higher than in the illustration of piaffe on the long reins.

assage; harmonic unison.